The

LOCAL CHURCH

Matters

The
LOCAL
CHURCH
Matters

Timothy Pigg

NORTHEASTERN BAPTIST PRESS

The Local Church Matters
Copyright © 2022 by Timothy Pigg

Published by Northeastern Baptist Press
Post Office Box 4600
Bennington, VT 05201

Cover design by Jared August and Leason Stiles

Paperback ISBN: 978-1-953331-19-9

I've known Timothy Pigg since he was a young boy and have observed his and his family's commitment to the local church. In *The Local Church Matters*, this young pastor eclipses his age and experience to give us a clear, concise, and clarion call to restore the local church to its biblical norm as the center of the Christian universe. This book's scriptural foundation, ministry wisdom, and practical helps make it a worthy tool for church leaders and members to use in being the people of God on Christ's mission.

Jim Shaddix

W. A. Criswell Chair of Expository Preaching
Southeastern Baptist Theological Seminary
Wake Forest, NC

A survey of the contents of Dr. Pigg's inaugural volume lets the reader know a blessing is ahead. *The Local Church Matters* is a comprehensive, biblically sound treatment of the New Testament Church. Especially helpful is Dr. Pigg's presentation of the office of pastor. I recommend this volume to all who want to follow the New Testament pattern in building a church today.

Jerry Vines

Two time President, Southern Baptist Convention
Pastor, First Baptist Church
Jacksonville, FL

In an age where pragmatics have become the priority, Timothy Pigg makes *The Local Church Matters* an accessible resource for believers who want to see the glory of the local church restored. With biblical foundations that find graceful application, not only does it refresh the pastor in fundamentals concerning the local church, it serves as a powerful bonding agent for local bodies as we make disciples together. If you are searching for a tool to strengthen or repair the foundation of discipleship in your church, I would highly recommend this work.

James Biesiadecki
Senior Pastor, First Baptist Church
Bartlesville, OK

Now, more than ever, Christians need clarity on the importance of the local church and how God has designed for it to function. Returning to the well-worn pages of the sufficient and authoritative Scriptures, Tim Pigg offers much needed clarity and biblical insight on why God's plan to rescue, redeem, and restore a fallen world takes place through the local expression called the Bride of Christ. This book is filled with biblical wisdom and leadership insights to help Christians cherish the local church the way our Savior does.

Daniel Dickard
Senior Pastor, Friendly Avenue Baptist Church
Greensboro, NC

I have known Timothy Pigg since he was a boy. His heart was in the local church then and as you will see in this volume it has never left. Come to a greater understanding of and a renewed commitment to your own local congregation as you journey through these pages because…The Local Church Still Matters!

O.S. Hawkins
Former Pastor of First Baptist Church in Dallas, TX
Author of the best selling Code *Series of Devotions*

The local church is a divine institution. It is the backbone of America and a centerpiece of all civilization. A local church—the gathered body of believers in a congregation—is an organization unlike any other. From the driver's seat of pastoral ministry in the context of the local church, Dr. Timothy Pigg offers an insightful and engaging look into what makes Christian churches exceptional in all of human history. Whether you are interested in joining a church, simply want to learn more, or find yourself curious as to why entire governments, secular institutions, educational establishments, and political leaders often are concerned by and oppose the work of the local church, this book is for you. A brief and engaging work, you will not want to put it down. Indeed, the local church matters!

Z. Scott Colter
Professor and Director or Strategic Initiatives
Mid-America Baptist Theological Seminary, Memphis, TN
Executive Director, Conservative Baptist Network
Partner, Colter & Co.

The local church, the Body of Christ, has been and continues to be God's chosen people for His work in this world, and in this Christ-commissioned work, it is all that matters. While Christian institutions fall pray to the siren songs of this world, while theologians fail to stay true to the Scriptures, and while the knees even of many local churches buckle under the weight of self-indulgence and failed philosophies, Timothy Pigg points the way for the local church that desires to matter in God's eyes. Walking through the Scriptures and tying biblical truths together in Christ-glorifying truth with plain sense interpretation, *The Local Church Matters* is a gift of simple explanation of the most profound teachings of God's Word for the church.

Waylan Owens

Dr. Timothy Pigg has provided a valuable resource for local church leaders and members. Writing out of a rich background of practical participation in and scholarly perspective on the local church, he offers a robust reminder of its strategic importance at a time when, sadly, individualism tends to overshadow community and personal experience eclipses doctrinal substance. Take up and read!

Matthew McKellar
Professor of Preaching | School of Theology
Southwestern Baptist Theological Seminary
Fort Worth, TX

Table of Contents

Chapter 1

Introduction

Why are you reading this book? Have you been thinking about getting back into church? Have you recently moved into a new community and find yourself looking for a church to attend? Are you a pastor or deacon looking to help your congregation understand what it means to be a church? No matter the reason you picked up this book, I hope that through reading it you will uncover the great design that God has for you through being a part of His church.

From my earliest memories as a child, I remember being in church. If the doors were open, Timothy Chad Pigg, was in church. My parents made sure of it. My mom and dad had no concept of going to church only on Sunday. On Sunday, we went to Sunday School and Worship Service;

then, in the evening, we came back for Training Union and another Worship Service. On Tuesday, we went out and did visitation, where we shared the gospel with the new visitors from the previous Sunday. We were back at church Wednesday for children's choir and Bible Study. When I was old enough to attend Youth Group, my parents would bring me to church on Friday and Saturday for discipleship training. You might think that going to church that much must have pushed me away, but actually the opposite happened. I love church! Something special happens when God's people gather God's way, according to God's Word, to do God's work. If you were to ask me, "Does the local church matter?" I would respond emphatically, "YES!"

Clive Staples (C.S.) Lewis in his book, *Screwtape's Letters*, underscores the truth that local churches matter. If you are unfamiliar with this particular work by Lewis, he is writing a fictional novel describing the unseen demonic world. Uncle Screwtape, as he is called in the book, is a ranking demon in the army of "Our Father Here Below" (i.e. Satan). His task is to oversee the work of his nephew, Wormwood. Wormwood has been assigned the task of keeping his "patient" (i.e. human) from ever believing by faith in Jesus for salvation from sin. As the story opens, Wormwood has failed at his one task, and thus finds himself scorned by his uncle as he looks for ways to stop the maturation of a young believer.

Among the hosts of tactics and schemes deployed by Screwtape and Wormwood, the one that is particularly cogent to this book is the ploy to utilize a local church as a means of destruction to a young believer. Screwtape remarks to his nephew Wormwood, "There is no need to despair; hundreds of these adult converts have been reclaimed after a brief sojourn in the Enemy's camp and are now with us. One of our great allies at the present is the Church itself."[1] How is it that a church could become an ally of Satan for the destruction of a believer? Most certainly the words of Screwtape to Wormwood would cause any person to be skeptical about ever stepping through the doors of a local church.

What we must understand is that the "ally" Screwtape is referring to is not the church of the New Testament for whom our Savior died, but rather an iteration, a façade of such establishment, which is most prevalent today. How do we know that Screwtape is not speaking of the thriving local churches that are recorded in Luke's narrative, the Acts of the Apostles? We know because Screwtape mentions his terror of such local churches. He continued by saying,

> Do not misunderstand me. I do not mean the Church as we see her spread out through all time and space and rooted in eternity, terrible as an army with banners. That, I confess, is a spectacle which makes our boldest tempters uneasy…All your patient sees is the half-finished, sham Gothic erection on the new building estate.[2]

As we can see, the "true" church (i.e. a local New Testament Church) is a great force to be reckoned with in any age.

There are two truths we can discern from Screwtape's statements about the church to his nephew. First, we learn that a functioning New Testament church squelches the fiery darts of Satan, and thus by Lewis's novel, he demonstrates the truthfulness of Jesus's statement to Peter in Matthew 16. Jesus told Peter, "the gates of Hell shall not prevail against [the church]" (Matthew 16:18). Second, we learn that a poorly functioning New Testament church provides a spark which ignites Satan's fiery darts to be aimed at immature believers to keep them from becoming a terror to Satan's plans.

Therefore, if a properly functioning New Testament church can bring terror to the prince of darkness, then the question becomes what does a properly functioning New Testament church look like today? That is precisely the question that I want to answer for you through this book, *The Local Church Matters*.

We are going to look at a host of topics that pertain to the local church. In chapter two, we will start with Jesus, who is the Lord and foundation of the church. In chapter three, we will look at who comprises the membership of the church. Can anyone be a member of a church? Is membership in a church like joining the local gym? In chapter four, we will explore the two ordinances, Baptism and Lord's Supper. Jesus gave these two ordinances to safeguard His church and help the church remain on mission. In chapter five, we will talk about the two offices of the church, pastor and deacon. God gave His church these offices as a gift to serve His church. In chapter six, we will look at the governance of the church and see how our local churches should be held accountable. In chapter seven, we will consider the mission of the church.

At the conclusion of each chapter, there will be a set of discussion questions. These discussion questions are designed to be used in a small group or a one-on-one setting. The purpose of these questions are to help you teach others that the local church matters. This book is designed to be used by pastors, church leaders, and church members. One suggested use of this book is for membership classes at your church.

Chapter 2

The Lord of the Church:
Jesus our Savior and Foundation

"And he is the head of the body, the church. He is the beginning, the firstborn from the dead, that in everything he might be preeminent."
Colossians 1:18

"For no one can lay a foundation other than that which is laid, which is Jesus Christ"
1 Corinthians 3:11

For all my life I have been amazed at people who have the gift of construction. This was not a gift that the Lord gave to me. My ability to build things is very limited. One Christmas, my wife and I were invited to enjoy dinner at a church member's home. Following dinner, the

7

husband and wife got out a gingerbread house kit for us to build. For what seemed like 2 hours, we worked to build a gingerbread house. I am embarrassed to tell you that we were unsuccessful. We could not get anything to stand up long enough to decorate. You could imagine the laughs we shared that night as our gingerbread house toppled over with every attempt.

Are you gifted at building things? Some people have a knack for building, and they have been that way all their life. At my church, we have a pastor on staff who is an engineer. He is a builder. His specialty is bridges. He understands how strong the foundation needs to be in order to support the weight of the concrete for the road and the cars that will travel along the bridge. I was talking to him one day about his job and he was sharing with me an important principle. This principle is simple, and I am sure you have heard it before. But for some reason, that day his statement grabbed my attention. Here is what he said, "Tim, your foundation matters." He went on to share about how the integrity of an entire structure is predicated on the strength of the foundation. This simple truth, *foundations matter*, certainly has implications for our discussion on the church.

The foundation of your church matters. The foundation of my church matters. Thankfully, we do not have to come up with our own blueprints in order to build a foundation for our churches. Instead, God has graciously given us His clear construction manual for how local congregations are to build the foundation of their church.

Just as my fellow pastor shared that simple principle that foundations matter, he also explained that the shape of your foundation determines the look of your building. Before we look at God's manual for building the foundation of a church, I want us to think about some of the foundations that churches build upon in our communities. Let's think about three of them that may be popular in your community: traditionalism, pragmatism, and consumerism. It is important for us to keep in mind that when we talk about foundations, we are talking about the base by which the entire congregation is built. The shape of the ministries, the scope of the outreach, and the substance of the preaching will all reveal the foundation.

Imagine you are driving along one Sunday morning and you pull into the parking lot of a church. The building harkens back memories of your earliest childhood as the outside façade is traditional. You get out of your car, walk up the stairs of the grand cathedral, pass the white columns, and through the massive wooden doors. You and your family sit down on the hard wooden pews near the back. The music is outdated, the pew Bible is the King James Version (KJV), the preacher is passionate, and the people are friendly.

After the Worship Service, you stop to talk to the pastor and ask him some questions. With every question you ask, the same response is given, "That's just how we have always done it here." That answer is not particularly alarming. What is alarming is when you begin to ask him, "why have you always done it that way?" His response or should I say his lack of response indicates the foundation of the church. He never mentions anything about the Bible. He never talks about Jesus being the foundation for any of the ministries or outreach that they do. He never talks about the Great Commission or the glory of God. Instead, what appears to be the foundation is *sacred* traditions of a once vibrant church that is now on life support.

Do you have a church in your community like that? If so, be careful. The foundation will soon crumble, and your family might become casualties of a faulty construction. The slogan of a church that is built upon the foundation of traditionalism is, "We have never done it that way before."

Concerned that your family might not locate a good church, you set out to find another church in town. You have done your research, and you have found a church that seems to be a "good fit" for your family. You visit their website and listen to the pastor's sermons on social media. The church looks great. The next Sunday you show up. After the Worship Service, you are convinced that this church is for you. The music is great, the message resonates with your heart, and your kids make friends immediately. You decide to keep going.

After being involved in this church for several months now, you begin to become uneasy about some of the changes that are happening. Not wanting to cause any issues in the church, you sit down with the church's leadership privately and share your concerns. Your desire is to hear them share biblical reasons for the changes that have been made. However, throughout the meeting not one leader shared a Bible verse. Instead, of hearing Bible verses you heard phrases like, "This new leadership book says we need to do church this way if we want to grow" or "the most popular church growth experts in our convention say that we need to stop doing these ministries if we want people to come." Dejected and discouraged, you leave the church because you realize that this particular congregation is not built upon the foundation of Jesus.

Have you ever been to a church like this one? A church who has pragmatism as their foundation. The pragmatic church lives by the mission statement, "We only do what works in our church." Be careful attending a church built on pragmatism. You will quickly find yourself abandoning the Bible for the principles of business and marketing in your life.

You have tried two churches in your community and both of them are built on a faulty foundation. Now, you are left wondering if your family will ever find a congregation of believers who are built upon the inerrancy and sufficiency of Scripture. However, you are determined to, "not forsake the assembling of yourself together" so you continue your church hunt (Heb. 10:25). It is now Easter week, and you receive a very attractive invitation in your mailbox about a church not too far from you.

Desperate for community and strong biblical teaching, you load your family in the car and you decide to attend the church that sent you the mailer. As you pull into the parking lot, the church sign strikes you as odd because the term "church" is nowhere to be found. The name of the church is Relevant Church, but only the word "relevant" is on the sign. You find the auditorium and take your seat about 5 minutes before the Worship Service is supposed to start. On the screens you notice a countdown clock. Once the clock hits zero, the lights go out and the stage lighting comes on. You immediately felt like you are attending a show meant to produce a wow rather than a service meant to lead you to worship. The music is good. The message is entertaining. But there is something missing. In a desire to be relevant, the church has washed out the bloodstains of the cross.

Ever been to a church like this? A church that has the foundation of consumerism. A consumeristic church is built on the foundation of the consumers (i.e. church members). The goal is to attract what the people want instead of doing what God wants. The preaching at a church built on consumerism becomes shallow because the pastor does not want to offend his membership. The need for repentance becomes too harsh and the gospel is abandoned for social reform.

The foundations of traditionalism, pragmatism, and consumerism promise the world, but leave you with nothing. Churches built upon these foundations cannot claim Jesus's promise in Matthew 16 that the gates of Hell will not prevail. Instead, of being a force of Kingdom advance in a community, a church built on any foundation outside of Scripture is an embassy for Satan.

Upon what foundation should the church be built? Simple, Jesus. Or to ask the question in a more theological way, "Who is Lord of the church?" It is important that every local church has Jesus as her foundation. Throughout this chapter, we are going to look at two churches: Corinth and Colossae. These two churches were reminded of the importance of having Jesus as their foundation.

The Lordship of Christ is the belief that Jesus is sovereign ruler over all things, and His sovereignty has implications for the church. The doctrine of the Lordship of Christ relates to our subject. The local church matters because it identifies the relationship the church has to Jesus. Thom Rainer, former President and CEO of Lifeway Christian Resources, identified the reasons that churches that are in decline continue the death march to extinction. He listed six perpetual behaviors of dying churches.[3] Each of the six behaviors that Rainer identified can be attributed to a misunderstanding of who is Lord of the church. Therefore, the Lordship of Christ being regularly practiced in the corporate body of the church is crucial for the health of the church.

Colossians 1:18–20: The Savior of the Church

One New Testament passage that teaches the Lordship of Christ is Colossians 1:15-18, in which Paul wrote,

> He is the image of the invisible God, the firstborn of all creation. For by him all things were created, in heaven and on earth, visible and invisible, whether thrones

or dominions or rulers or authorities—all things were created through him and for him. And he is before all things, and in him all things hold together. And he is the head of the body, the church. He is the beginning, the firstborn from the dead, that in everything he might be preeminent.

Paul outlined in this passage that Jesus, because He is the "firstborn of all creation," sits as the Lord of the church. Daniel Akin explained, "These verses constitute a Christ-hymn exalting the Son as the supreme Lord."[4]

Paul recognizes the enthronement of Jesus's Lordship in Colossians 1:18 where he says that, "[Jesus] is the head of the body, the church" (Col. 1:18). Akin noted, "The church owes [Jesus] exclusive allegiance, complete devotion, and total obedience."[5] Everything in your church and my church should f from the fact that Jesus is the Lord of the church.

What has Jesus accomplished that gives Him such an elite status to demand exclusive allegiance? Paul answered that very question in Colossians 1:18b where he described Jesus as, "the firstborn of the dead" (Col. 1:18b). This phrase, "firstborn of the dead" speaks to Jesus having conquered our greatest foe, death, through His bodily resurrection. Akin noted the, "resurrection is His claim to be head of the church."[6] Therefore, as head of the church, Jesus has the right and authority to set the criteria by which a local church functions and operates.

1 Corinthians 3:11: The Foundation of the Church

Just as the Colossians needed a reminder that Jesus is the Savior of the church, so too the Corinthians needed a similar reminder that Jesus is the foundation of the church. Paul reminded the Corinthians and us that, "For no one can lay a foundation other than that which is laid, which is Jesus Christ." These words by Paul are striking. He makes a very narrow and exclusive claim about what constitutes a church. He claims that only the gatherings that have Jesus as their foundation meet the criteria necessary to be called a church. Any other gathering that claims to be a church without Jesus as their foundation is a false church.

The local church matters. The foundation of your church and my church matters. It is paramount that we make sure that Jesus is the one who is enthroned in our churches. We must consciously submit to Christ's leadership in every area of our church and personal life. The local church mattered enough to Jesus that He died for her; therefore, she should matter enough to us to keep Jesus as the foundation.

Discussion Questions:

1. Where have you seen traditionalism, pragmatism, and consumerism in the churches that you have attended?

2. What does it mean to have Jesus as the foundation of the church?

3. Has Jesus been made the foundation of your life? If not, visit this website: www.thegreatestnews.org.

Chapter 3

Members of the Church:
Regenerate Church Membership

*"So those who received his word were baptized, and there
were added that day about three thousand souls."*
Acts 2:41

*"And day by day, attending the temple together and breaking bread
in their home, they received their food with glad and generous hearts,
praising God and having favor with all the people. And the Lord added to their number day by day those who were being saved."*
Acts 2:46-47

Having just graduated with my Master of Divinity at Southwestern Baptist Theological Seminary, my wife and I loaded up our car and moved from Fort Worth, TX to Immokalee, FL in May 2015. First Baptist Church of Immokalee is a congregation that I think is typical of most Southern Baptist churches that have a long history. Our congregation experienced "glory days" and "dry seasons." There is one story I will never forget.

It was Sunday, May 17, 2015, my first Sunday as the pastor of First Baptist Church of Immokalee. My nerves were beyond tense as I thought about the great responsibility of shepherding God's church. The sermon was ready, the bulletins were printed, and I was prayed-up as I waited for God's people to show up. We had wonderful attendance that first Sunday. If my memory serves me correctly there were 88 people in attendance. During the greeting portion of the service, family after family came up to me to let me know how excited they were that I was their pastor. Families shared with me that they had been members of the church for decades. I had several families that had been members of the church for over 50 years. On our way to lunch after church, I remember looking at my wife and telling her that God is going to do something special here.

However, everything that was so glorious on Sunday, May 17, 2015, went away on Sunday, May 24, 2015. What happened in one week? For starters, all the members who were there the previous week did not show back up the following Sunday. In one week, the church attendance dropped from 88 people to less than 45 people. How can a church split in just 7 days? Was it something that I preached? As weeks, months, and years went by, my chairman of deacons, Bill, and I visited every family in the church. In our visits, we pleaded with members to come back to church. We shared testimonies about what God was doing at the church, we shared Scripture passages with them that speak about the importance of being at church for spiritual growth. We told them about how God has gifted them to be in service at the church. It seemed like the more we pleaded and begged the less interested these "church members" were in being part of the church.

After two years of hard work to no avail, the Lord taught me an important lesson. The lesson that I learned was that if the local church matters, then regenerate church membership matters too. Having a church membership list that has hundreds of people on it that do not come to church is like walking into a morgue and calling it the nursery of a hospital; there are bodies but no life.

A pastor friend of mine described the epidemic of un-regenerate church membership with this following question, "How do you know you are alive; is it because you have a birth certificate? No. You are alive because you are breathing, and your heart is beating." The point he was making was that many people believe they are alive spiritually because they have their name on the church membership roll. However, the reality is the breath of God has never awakened their spirit as evidenced through repentance and faith. This chapter is going to make the case that regenerate church membership is biblical and therefore essential if the local church is going to matter. J.L. Reynolds, former pastor of Second Baptist Church in Richmond, Virginia in the 1800s commented, "It is, therefore, the imperative duty of the Churches to admit to membership none but such as give satisfactory evidence that they have been born again."[7] In order for the local church to matter, the membership must be followers of Christ.

Developing a biblical understanding for regenerate church membership can be found through three biblical passages: Matthew 16:15-20, Matthew 18:15-20, and Acts 15. These three passages will provide the scope and application of regenerate church membership in the context of a local church.

MATTHEW:
THE FOUNDATION AND MAINTENANCE
OF REGENERATE CHURCH MEMBERSHIP

Matthew, in his gospel, underscored the importance of regenerate church membership through two passages, Matthew 16 and Matthew 18. Interestingly, Matthew is the only gospel writer to use the word "church" in his gospel. In Matthew 16:18 Jesus provided the foundation for church membership in the story concerning Peter's confession of Jesus as the Messiah. In Matthew 18:15-20, Jesus provided the key to maintaining regenerate church membership through His explanation on how to restore a sinful church member. These two passages in Matthew 16:18 and Matthew 18:17 provide the theological groundwork for the concept of regenerate church membership.

First, in Matthew 16, Jesus wanted to get the general consensus of the people concerning His identity. He posited a question to His disciples. His question, "Who do people say that I am?" garnered responses that did not speak to Jesus's true identity as the Messiah. Therefore, Jesus turned to His disciples and asked the question in a more personal way. "Who do you say that I am?" It was this question, and the subsequent answer by Simon that Jesus used to explain that the foundation of the church is the right confession of its members as to the identity of Jesus. Peter's response, "You are the Christ, the Son of the Living God" garnered from Jesus a new name for Simon, and an explanation of the foundation of a church. Malcom Yarnell points out one critical observation about this passage in his edited book, *Upon This Rock*. He said, "Simon is renamed because he no longer spoke about a revelation as a distant matter; rather, Simon now received that revelation as his own and confessed it personally as a profound reality. Simon's Christian name is now Peter."[8]

The changing of Simon's name to Peter (Grk. Πετρος) and the following words of Jesus that the church would be built upon a rock (Grk. Πετρα) demonstrated Matthew's use of wordplay to communicate that the foundation of the church is Jesus Christ rightly confessed by a regenerate believer. Therefore, this example from Matthew 16 provides an example of regenerate church membership by Jesus's pronouncement that He will build His church.

If God's standard for church membership is that every person on a church membership roll be regenerate, then how does a congregation protect itself from having unregenerate people join their church and remain members? The maintenance of regenerate church membership is through church discipline, which is explained in Matthew 18. Jesus, in Matthew 18:17, uses the word "church" to describe the relationship between Christians. John Nolland explained, "In practical terms the teaching of 18:15–17 will be worked out in relation to an individual Christian congregation which is one of many such congregations."[9]

Jesus explained that failure of the sinful Christian to repent would result in his expulsion from the church and him being marked as a "Gentile and a tax collector" (Matt. 18:17). These two descriptions by Jesus demonstrate the groundwork for regenerate church membership. The "Gentile and tax collector" reference were monikers used by Matthew for people who were not Christians.[10] Leon Morris explained Matthew's reference of "Gentile and tax collector" in this way when he said, "these expressions stand for people outside the people of God, people who have sinned and not repented."[11] Morris's position that Matthew's reference of "Gentile and tax collector" indicates that the person is not a believer is also articulated by Craig Blomberg in his New American Commentary on Matthew's gospel. Blomberg said, "To treat a person as a 'pagan or a tax collector' means to treat him or her as unredeemed and outside the Christian community."[12] Blomberg and Morris demonstrate through their understanding of Matthew's reference of "Gentile and tax collector" that those who are called the church are the ones who are regenerate.

ACTS:
THE DISPUTE ABOUT WHO CAN BE
A CHURCH MEMBER

Luke told a story that has implications for the discussion concerning regenerate church membership. The story of the Jerusalem Council in Acts 15 provides evidence for regenerate church membership through confirming that entrance into the church is by faith and not through works. There are three implications that can be made concerning regenerate church membership from the decision made by the Jerusalem Counsel. First, church membership is accessible by the completed atoning work of Jesus on the cross. Second, church membership is available to anyone who has the indwelling of the Holy Spirit. Third, church membership is evidenced through regenerate behavior, which stems from a regenerate heart.

Church Membership Is Accessible
Because of Jesus

Without the atoning sacrifice of Jesus applied by faith to the heart of a repentant person, there is no access of fellowship that would constitute church membership. It was that conclusion concerning salvation that Paul and Barnabas were lobbying Peter and James about during the Jerusalem Council. The teaching that was being confronted by Paul and Barnabas was mentioned in Acts 15:5, which said, "But some believers who belonged to the party of the Pharisees rose up and said, 'It is necessary to circumcise them and to order them to keep the law of Moses.'" In essence, what was being taught was that church membership and cooperation was only accessible to those who were keepers of the law. Therefore, it was not the atoning sacrifice of Jesus that brought fellowship (i.e. church membership), but righteousness according to the Law. However, James, the Apostles, and the entire Church at Jerusalem determined that the Scripture is clear. Salvation is not received by keeping the Law, but regeneration comes by grace through faith in Jesus alone. Therefore, the implication is that church membership, identifying with other people that you are a Christ follower, is only for those who are saved by faith.

Church Membership Is Available to Anyone Indwelt by the Holy Spirit

A second implication concerning regenerate church membership is found in Acts 15. That implication was noted in Acts 15:8-9, which said, "And God, who knows the heart, bore witness to them, by giving them the Holy Spirit just as He did to us, and He made no distinction between us and them, having cleansed their hearts by faith." The second implication is that church membership is available to any person with the indwelling of the Holy Spirit because to have the indwelling of the Holy Spirit is a testimony of salvation.[13]

Church Membership is Identifiable by Regenerate Behavior

A third implication can be made concerning regenerate church membership from the Jerusalem Council incident of Acts 15. The third implication is that regenerate membership is the only membership type that can expect regenerate actions. Acts 15:19-20 outlined the expected behaviors that would be practiced regularly in the life of a regenerate church member. Confirmation of the truth that a regenerate heart does regenerate actions is found through the teachings of Jesus in Matthew 12:33-37 and Mark 7:14-23 and through the teachings of the Apostles in James 3:13, Ephesians 2:1-10, and Galatians 5:16-26.

In conclusion, regenerate church membership is essential for a local church to matter. It separates those that attend Worship Services in two categories, the church and the lost. Having this clarification is important for how a church practices the ordinances, which we will cover in the next chapter.

DISCUSSION QUESTIONS:

1. What has been your experience with church membership?

2. What is the biblical criteria of church membership?

3. Should church membership be withheld from a person who professes Christ, but has a lifestyle that is in conflict with biblical teaching?

Chapter 4

The Ordinances of the Church: Baptism and the Lord's Supper

"We were buried therefore with him by baptism into death, in order that, just as Christ was raised from the dead by the glory of the Father, we too might walk in newness of life."
Romans 6:4

"For as often as you eat this bread and drink the cup, you proclaim the Lord's death until he comes."
1 Corinthians 11:26

Ever since I was a little boy growing up in church, the ordinances of baptism and the Lord's Supper were intriguing to me. At First Baptist Church of Jacksonville, we would routinely have baptisms on Sunday night. I can remember sitting in church watching as 5, 10, or even 20 people were being baptized at the start of the Worship Service. At times, it seemed that the baptisms took forever. The lights would dim at the start of the Worship Service, and our attention was drawn to the baptismal.

Also, throughout the year, we would take the Lord's Supper. Before I had professed Christ as my personal Lord and Savior, I used to sit next to my grandmother, and she would explain to me the importance of the Lord's Supper. Of course, because I was not yet a Christian, my grandmother withheld the bread and the cup from me, but I remember vividly the Bible lesson that I received from her every time our church took the Lord's Supper. It was frustrating to have to sit there and observe the Lord's Supper and not be allowed to partake. However, the withholding of the Lord's Supper was something that God used in my life to draw me unto himself by faith and repentance. Therefore, once I believed by faith and was forgiven of my sin, the first time that I partook of the Lord's Supper was a special occasion that I will never forget.

This chapter is going to address the two ordinances that Jesus assigned to be practiced by his church as a memorial to his death, burial, and resurrection. The act of these two ordinances is important for the spiritual health of a local church. Baptism is the front door of the church and the Lord's Supper helps to keep the body of Christ in good spiritual shape.

Baptism

One day that I will never forget as a pastor was the Sunday morning that I performed my first baptism and someone about drowned.

I received little sleep the night before and I arrived at the church early to make sure everything was ready. As soon as I walked into the sanctuary and saw the baptismal was full, my palms began to sweat, and my heart began to race. I walked up to the baptismal and leaned over to feel if the water was warm. Just at that moment my cell phone slid out of my shirt pocket and went to the bottom of the pool. If being nervous was not enough, I had now ruined my new cell phone. Not able to worry about replacing my phone, I turned my attention to getting ready for the baptism.

The service began and the worship minister directed everyone's attention to the baptismal. There I was with everyone looking at me. At the start, I explained to everyone about how exciting it was for us to celebrate baptism as a church. I then invited the high school student to join me in the baptismal waters. At that time, I said all the typical phrases that a pastor would normally say. Then I lowered my baptismal candidate under the water, and it was at that moment that I became overcome with the novelty of doing my first baptism that I forgot to bring up the person from immersion. It was not until that baptismal candidate opened their eyes that I knew that I had forgotten to raise them up. I quickly raised them up. I could not escape that moment fast enough. All I wanted to do was hide my face from the congregation. Seriously, what pastor forgets to raise up their baptismal candidate on their first baptism? Thankfully, in God's providence, He has been good to me to allow me ample opportunities to correct my mistake.

You know what was the worst mistake from performing my first baptism? It was not that I forgot to bring the baptismal candidate back up in a timely manner. Actually, my worst mistake from performing my first baptism was that I failed to properly explain the ordinance of baptism to the congregation.

I truly believe that many in our churches have observed the ordinance of baptism but fail to understand the true significance of baptism. God has provided to His church the ordinance of baptism to show forth that the local church matters. To show that baptism matters, three questions are going to be answered: 1) What is baptism?, 2) Who can be baptized?, and 3) How should baptism be practiced?

WHAT IS BAPTISM?

The first question that I want us to consider is, what is baptism? Simply put, baptism is an ordinance of the local church, by which a believer publicly identifies with Jesus's death, burial, and resurrection.

Now, let's look at this definition more closely. *Baptism is an ordinance of the local church.* This means that the practice of baptism is to be conducted through the ministry of a local church. Baptism is not an event that happens outside the confines of a local church's authority. The ordinance by virtue of it's nature is for the local church.

In addition, baptism is an ordinance of the local church, *by which a believer publicly identifies with Jesus*. This means that baptism is an action of outward obedience caused by inward regeneration. Throughout the New Testament the act of baptism was a public ordeal. For instance, Jesus's baptism was done publicly by John the Baptist in the Jordan River. Another, example was the baptism of the Ethiopian in Acts that was performed publicly by Philip.

Finally, baptism is an ordinance of the local church, by which a believer publicly identifies with Jesus's *death, burial, and resurrection*. The act of baptism displays the work of the gospel that Jesus accomplished. Paul supplies the understanding that baptism symbolizes Jesus's death, burial, and resurrection in Romans 6:4, which says, "We were buried therefore with him by baptism into death, in order that, just as Christ was raised from the dead by the glory of the Father, we too might walk in newness of life."

WHO CAN BE BAPTIZED?

The second question we need to consider is who can be baptized? To answer this question, I want to tell you about a group of 16th Century believers who saw the ordinance of baptism to be of such importance that they were willing to face death for their beliefs. Many of these faithful brothers and sisters were burned, beheaded, or provided their "permanent baptism" (to drown) for holding to the New Testament understanding that baptism is an ordinance of the church only to be administered upon a person who has rightly confessed Christ through repentance and faith. Some have even estimated that the average lifespan of an Anabaptist was 18-months after he was biblically baptized as a believer by immersion. These believers are known as the Anabaptist. These Anabaptist were killed because of how they answered the question, who can be baptized?

Who can be baptized? The only person who is biblically qualified to be a participant in the ordinance of baptism is a believer. It is an ordinance reserved only for those who have by faith trusted in the completed work of Christ on the cross for the forgiveness of sin and has evidenced such faith through a desire of repentance. This definition of believer's baptism is quite narrow. For instance, it excludes everyone who is not a confessing believer. The practice of pedobaptism (infant baptism) is not true baptism at all. Therefore, religious groups like Presbyterians, Episcopalians, and Roman Catholics, who practice infant baptism, would not meet the New Testament criteria for their practice of baptism.

How Should Baptism Be Practiced?

The third question, how should baptism be practiced, is addressing the actual act of baptism. In theological circles, this question would be framed as follows, what is the proper mode of baptism? What I want us to consider is does the

Bible have anything to say regarding how a person should be baptized? The Bible is very clear about how a baptism is to be practiced. To understand how baptism is to be carried out in the context of a local church we need to understand the linguistic and theological argument.

The linguistic argument for how baptism is to be practiced is simple. The term "baptism" is a transliteration of a word that is used frequently in the New Testament. Now, by transliteration, I mean that it is a word that sounds very similar to the original Greek word. The New Testament Greek word for baptism is *baptizo.* The definition of baptism is "to immerse under water." Therefore, to baptize properly one must immerse the entire body under water.

The theological argument for how baptism is to be practiced is that it must reflect the death, burial, and resurrection. In John 10, Jesus describes his death as laying down his life (John 10:11, 15, 17-18). The act of lowering a baptismal candidate under the water signifies the death and burial of Jesus. Furthermore, the baptismal candidate is identifying himself as dying to his sin nature (Rom. 6:4, Gal. 2:20). The act of raising the baptismal candidate out of the water signifies the glorious resurrection of Jesus from the dead. The symbolism of the resurrection also applies to the believer because as Romans 6:4 explains believers not only identify with Jesus's death, but also his resurrection.

Therefore, linguistically and theologically the only mode of baptism that is appropriate to express the gospel is a baptism by full immersion. Any other such baptism is really no baptism at all. Considering these two arguments, this would mean that any church that fails to practice baptism by immersion is not accurately portraying the ordinance of baptism.

Lord's Supper

After completing my seminars in the doctoral program at Southwestern Baptist Theological Seminary, it became time for me to decide on a topic for my dissertation. I knew that I wanted to write on the local church, but I was not sure of my topic. I remember having a conversation with my parents' pastor at that time, Dr. Hayes Wicker. Wicker served at First Baptist Church of Naples for over 25 years. You could describe his ministry in southwest Florida as successful. His success was not evidenced because First Baptist Church of Naples was big, but his ministry was successful because of the centrality of repentance that was practiced regularly in the life of the church.

During a meeting, I asked him what contributed to the peace and unity that First Baptist Church of Naples had experienced during his pastorate. His answer was simple, "The Lord's Supper." Curious at his response, I inquired further. Ultimately, he shared with me that a tool God has given to His church to maintain unity and purity is the ordinance of the Lord's Supper. He explained that taking the Lord's Supper monthly allowed the congregation to regularly address personal sin. Therefore, by addressing sin regularly the congregation maintained their focus on loving God, loving each other, and loving the lost. My curiosity peaked at this response and desiring to study more intently on the connection between the Lord's Supper and biblical unity in a local church, I began my research. That conversation led ultimately to my dissertation on church revitalization from 1 Corinthians.

I want to share with you why the ordinance of the Lord's Supper matters for your church. Throughout this section, it will be argued that a proper practice of the Lord's Supper will produce unity and "togetherness" among the congregation. True biblical fellowship matters and the Lord's Supper will help a local church to achieve that goal.

I think you will agree with me that the divisiveness among churches is astonishing. New church plants are beginning, at times, as a result of church splits. I know my own church, prior to my arrival in May 2015, boasted of planting four churches in their community. You could imagine the excitement to hear of such a missional congregation. However, after learning more through reading my congregation's business meeting notes, it became evident that these four church plants were not because of being mission-minded, but rather it was the consequence of various church splits.

Church splits can have several causes. One possible cause of church division is the lack of biblical clarity from the pulpit. According to a recent report produced by the Barna Group entitled "The State of the Church 2016," the majority of church goers believe that good works are a sufficient method for attaining eternal life.[14] Another possible cause of church division is the lack of understanding concerning ethical truth. The rise of relativism promotes an individualistic mindset that is void of thinking about the whole; thus an unhealthy rise of the individual can lead to the demise of the community. More causes for church splits and division can be listed, and I am sure that you likely have heard of stories yourself, so the question before us is…what is the solution to such fragmentation in the church?

The solution is for local churches to once again recover that the biblical ordinance of the Lord's Supper matters. It is my opinion that a correct administration of the Lord's Supper will produce a gathering that can be characterized by the term, "together." Four times in 1 Corinthians 11:17-34, Paul uses the term, "together." In order to defend the claim that the Lord's Supper matters for the local church because it produces "togetherness" (i.e. fellowship), we will need to look at two headings, which are derived from 1 Corinthians 11: 1) A Divided Gathering and 2) Displaying Togetherness.

A Divided Gathering

Paul explains in 1 Corinthians 11:17-22, that the assembling of the Corinthian church was detrimental to their spiritual health because they were misusing the Lord's Supper. Think about that proposition for just a moment. Is it not a sad state for the church when it's gathering is spiritually unhealthy for a believer?

Let's look at Paul's remarks in 1 Corinthians 11:2 and 11:17 to see the stark contrast. In 1 Corinthians 11:2, Paul "commends" the Corinthians for their faithfulness to the traditions that he delivered to them. However, his tone changes quickly to sorrow in 11:17 when he says, "I do not commend you." Paul's shift in tone comes from his astonishment that when the church gathers there is divisiveness. Cole explains,

> The disorder at Corinth, when they gathered to eat and remember Christ's sacrifice, was a consequence of the disregard shown to other members of the body. This disregard, in my view, was how Christ's "body and blood" (his historic sacrifice) was despised at Corinth.[15]

Paul provides two indictments against the Corinthian church concerning their gatherings, which demonstrates their division and lack of regard for each other and the administration of the Lord's Supper.

Divided Social Groups

The first indictment that Paul has with the Corinthian church is that they are divided according to social groups. The term Paul uses in 1 Corinthians 11:18 to express their division is σχισμα. This particular term is used only 6 times in the New Testament, and three of those usages are by Paul in 1 Corinthians.

In order for us to understand what Paul means by "division," we need to look at his usages throughout 1 Corinthians. The first usage of the term "division," by Paul is in 1 Corinthians 1:10, which says, "I appeal to you, brothers, by the name of our Lord Jesus Christ, that all of you agree, and that there be no divisions among you, but that you be united in the same mind and the same judgment." Paul outlines in 1 Corinthians 1:10 how he will use the term "division" throughout the letter. The term "division" stands in stark contrast to three admonitions. Those admonitions are to "agree," "same mind," and "same judgment." Therefore, Paul is explaining that division is what occurs when people are not in unity with one another. The second and third usage of "division" are located in 1 Corinthians 11. Paul reiterates his definition of division by using a contrasting term of "together." Being "together" is the opposite of "division."

Understanding that the term "division" is used by Paul to show how the church has disunity, it becomes important for us to recognize what produced the division in the church. The division in the Corinthian church comes from their unhealthy understanding of social distinctions and petty alienations of feeling.[16] Paul condemns the social elitism in 1 Corinthians 11:22, where he says, "Do you not have houses to eat and drink in? Or do you despise the church of God and humiliate those who have nothing?" Wiersbe says, "Another fault was selfishness: the rich people brought a great deal of food for themselves while the poorer members went hungry."[17] The Corinthian church was clearly divided into social classes of the "haves and haves not." The social elites in the Corinthian church placed their personal desires above that of the entire congregation. The result of such practice was a divided congregation that defiled the divinely inspired ordinance of the Lord's Supper. To the social elites, the Lord's Supper did not matter.

Divided Biblical Teaching

The second indictment that Paul gives the Corinthian church is that they are following heresy. Paul said in 1 Corinthians 11:19, "there must be factions among you…". The factions concerning doctrinal heresy demonstrated the spiritual ineptness in the Corinthian church. Local congregations will struggle with seeing that the Lord's Supper matters when their congregations are in serious doctrinal decline.

Therefore, the question becomes, what heretical tenets are the Corinthians holding as their orthodox doctrine? Providing an answer to this question is difficult because the immediate context of chapter 11 does not give any clear indication. However, in 1 Corinthians 15, Paul does address a heretical teaching concerning the gospel. All of 1 Corinthians 15 is Paul's admonition to the Corinthian believers to hold to a right understanding of the gospel.

Paul outlines in 1 Corinthians 11:17-22 two major downfalls of the Corinthian church. They were divided over social status and they were divided over heretical teaching. These downfalls brought about great disappointment to Paul. Also, the social divide and the apparent heresies produced a church that was not administering the Lord's Supper in a manner that was beneficial to everyone. Therefore, Paul's indictment turns into a warning for the church to not bring judgment upon themselves because they have defiled the Lord's Supper and have not been "together" in their purpose (1 Cor. 11:29).

Displaying Togetherness

Now that we have looked at the spiritual concerns that inhibited the Corinthians from upholding a proper practice of the Lord's Supper, let's turn our attention to why the Lord's Supper matters for the local church. To explain how the Lord's Supper matters to the local church, we will need to look at the term "together." Being together means that individual people have assembled to form a group that has a unified intended purpose which leads to their new identity as a church. In 1 Corinthians, the misappropriation and administration of the Lord's Supper was a contributing factor in the church not being characterized by their "togetherness." Michael Haykin says that the Lord's Supper should be taken by, "happy members of the same family of faith and love."[18] Pendleton, in his book, *Baptist Church Manual*, argues that the Lord's Supper should, "express [the church's] Christian fellowship."[19] Therefore, Paul undertakes the responsibility to call the people back to a unified purpose in their gathering through reinstating a biblical observance of the Lord's Supper and helping the Corinthians see that the Lord's Supper matters.

THREE INSTRUCTIONS FOR TAKING THE LORD'S SUPPER

Paul gives three instructions in 1 Corinthians 11:23-34 to show why the Lord's Supper matters. These three instructions are to explain Christ, examine the heart, and exercise humility.

Explain Christ

The first instruction Paul gives is for the church to explain Christ in verses 23-26. The chief responsibility of the Lord's Supper is to be the proclamation of the gospel. Why does the Lord's Supper matter? It matters because the gospel matters!

Paul takes the Corinthians back to the Divine Word in order to regain a biblical understanding of the Lord's Supper and to explain the correct administration of the Lord's Supper in order to unite the church under their intended purpose. Paul appeals, not to his apostleship for authority, but he makes his instruction upon what has been passed to him by the Lord (1 Cor. 11:23). Pendleton explains that the church should, "look to the New Testament rather than human tradition for guidance" about how she should administer the Lord's Supper.[20] I think we can all give Pendleton a hearty, "Amen" with his sentiment that the Lord's Supper is a New Testament ordinance and not a human tradition. Therefore, Paul's instruction is authoritative because it comes directly from God.

Paul advocates two aspects of Christ that need to be explained if the church is going to proclaim the gospel. The first is the physical agony of the cross portrayed through the breaking of bread, and the second is the atonement produced by the cross through the taking of the cup. Both of these pictorials serve as memorials to the accomplishments Christ procured on the cross for sinners.

The symbolism and implications of the bread for the Lord's Supper matter. The bread symbolizes the broken body of Jesus. Several implications for the local church of Jesus's broken body being personified through the taking of bread is that through Jesus's body we find nutrition and unity in the church. Just as bread gives nutrition for our physical bodies, so too does Jesus provide for us spiritual life. Therefore, through the taking of the bread, the church is reminded that spiritual health comes only through Jesus. Furthermore, the bread symbolizes the unity Jesus provides to His church. This unity is shown through Jesus taking one loaf and distributing it to each person. Therefore, the symbolism of bread proclaims that Christ's body being broken was necessary for sinners to receive unity with God and the spiritual nutrition to refresh a life that is dead in sin (Eph. 2).

The second symbol Paul explains is the taking of the cup. The importance of the cup is to demonstrate the new covenant inaugurated by Jesus through His blood. In the New Testament, Christ's blood refers to one's new life in Christ. It is only through blood that remission of sin is possible. Hebrews 9:22 explains, "Indeed, under the law almost everything is purified with blood, and without the shedding of blood there is no forgiveness of sins." Paul's explanation of the elements of the bread and cup indicates that the first intention of the Lord's Supper is the proclamation of the gospel.

Examine Your Heart

The second instruction Paul gives for a local church in the administration of the Lord's Supper is to examine their spiritual maturity. This instruction is preventative and enables the congregation to avoid being guilty, "concerning the body and blood of the Lord" (1 Cor. 11:27). Paul gives this instruction through explaining the purpose of God's judgment upon a believer's life.

While the taking of the Lord's Supper is important, how a believer takes the Lord's Supper is also important. Paul's instruction for the church to examine their heart before taking the Lord's Supper is a command. It is a mandate from God that every time the Lord's Supper is administered there must be an opportunity for examination. Therefore, examining your own spiritual genuineness of heart to see if you are living in accordance to God's instruction is essential if the Lord's Supper is going to matter.

The consequences are devastating for failing to examine your heart correctly. Paul explains that God's judgment rests upon those who fail to correctly examine their heart before taking the Lord's Supper. God's judgement comes in the form of physical malady towards the offender. Paul explains three possible outcomes for a believer who examines incorrectly. The first outcome is weakness. The second outcome is illness. The final outcome for a believer who has done a poor job of examining his life accordingly is death. Paul is not speaking of eternal death, in the sense that man becomes separated from God, but rather physical death. Paul interprets these consequences as being acts of God's grace. He says, "But when we are judged by the Lord, we are disciplined so that we may not be condemned along with the world" (1 Cor. 11:32). Judgment from God on earth is better than judgment from God in heaven.

Exercise Humility

The final instruction that Paul gives to the Corinthian church for how they should administer the Lord's Supper and produce unity in their gathering is through exercising humility. The command of humility is communicated through the second to last imperative in the pericope. Paul calls the Corinthians to "wait" (11:33). The calling to wait communicates that every believer is equal. No more can the social elites consume the food prior to the rest of the church arriving. Now everyone must eat together and thus demonstrate their unity of purpose.

CONCLUSION

The struggle of many churches is the unity of the church body. Paul addresses a church that has been disruptive in the mission and divided in their gatherings. To correct this atrocity, Paul calls for a recovery of the biblical term "together." His steps of recovery include the right administration of the Lord's Supper. Therefore, Paul's solution for how the church can recover a biblical understanding of being together is through the right administration of the Lord's Supper. Because the local church matters, the Lord's Supper also matters.

DISCUSSION QUESTIONS:

1. Is infant baptism an acceptable practice for a church considering what the New Testament teaches concerning what baptism symbolizes?

2. Does believer's baptism have to be by immersion to be a legitimate baptism?

3. Should congregations withhold the Lord's Supper from members who are flagrantly living in sin?

4. Is it acceptable to practice the ordinances of baptism and the Lord's Supper outside the setting of a local church?

Chapter 5

The Servants of the Church: Pastors and Deacons

"And he gave the apostles, the prophets, the evangelists, the shepherds and teachers, to equip the saints for the work of ministry, for building up the body of Christ, until we all attain to the unity of the faith and of the knowledge of the Son of God, to mature manhood, to the measure of the stature of the fullness of Christ..."
Ephesians 4:11-13

"For those who serve well as deacons gain a good standing for themselves and also great confidence in the faith that is in Christ Jesus."
1 Timothy 3:13

L eadership is important. When we think about leadership, we think about the person who is at the top of an organizational chart. We think about the person who has all the authority. We think about managers, C.E.O's, owners, etc. However, when we read our Bibles we learn something about leadership that is counter-cultural. We learn that leadership is not about being first.

The greatest leader the world has ever seen is without question, Jesus. His impact upon the world is unprecedented. When the Bible describes His leadership, we are introduced to humility not exaltation. In Philippians 2, Paul describes the mind of Jesus that should be in every believer. He said,

> Have this mind among yourselves, which is yours in Christ Jesus, who, though He was in the form of God, did not count equality with God a thing to be grasped, but *emptied* Himself, by taking the form of a servant, being born in the likeness of men. And being found in human form, He *humbled* Himself by becoming obedient to the point of death, even death on a cross. Therefore God has highly *exalted* Him and bestowed on Him the name that is above every name (Phil. 2:5-9).[21]

The proper posture of a leader in a church is that of a servant. Why? Because that is the posture of Jesus. He was a servant; therefore, leaders of His church must also be servants.

This chapter is going to look at the two servant-leaders of the church: pastor and deacon. The role of the pastor will be considered first. Questions that will be answered in this section will include: Who is qualified to serve as a pastor? Can women be pastors? What does a pastor do? The role of a deacon will be considered second. We will look at the need for deacons and their qualifications and ministry.

Pastor

The role of the pastor is to lead a local church. However, the manner by which the pastor is called to lead is nuanced by three terms that are used interchangeably in the New Testament to speak of the office of the pastor. These three words are bishop, elder, and pastor. There are two locations in the New Testament where all three of these terms are used to describe the local church office of pastor. The first location is Acts 20:17-38 where Paul exhorts the pastors of the Ephesians. The second is 1 Peter 5:1-5 where Peter encourages the pastors of the Dispersion to remain faithful to the Lord amid their suffering. In this section, we are going to look at the qualifications of a pastor and the function of a pastor.

A Pastor's Qualifications

Is every believer qualified to serve as a pastor? The answer to that question is—no. God has given to his church a list of qualifications that are to be descriptive of the person that occupies the office of pastor. You could say that God's qualifications are the character requirements necessary to be considered as a candidate for serving as a pastor.

You can find these qualifications in 1 Timothy 3 and Titus 1. Let's look at 1 Timothy 3:1-7 for our consideration of these qualifications:

> The saying is trustworthy: If anyone aspires to the office of overseer, he desires a noble task. [2] Therefore an overseer must be above reproach, the husband of one wife, sober-minded, self-controlled, respectable, hospitable, able to teach, [3] not a drunkard, not violent but gentle, not quarrelsome, not a lover of money. [4] He must manage his own household well, with all dignity keeping his children submissive, [5] for if someone does not know how to manage his own household, how will he care for God's church? [6] He must not be a recent convert, or he may become puffed up with conceit and fall into the condemnation of the devil. [7] Moreover, he must be well thought of by outsiders, so that he may not fall into disgrace, into a snare of the devil (1 Tim. 3:1-7).

As you can tell, God takes the character of a pastor seriously. Of the fifteen qualifications listed, thirteen of them have something to say about the godliness of the individual. The only two qualifications that do not deal with a virtue explicitly, but rather speak of a function are "able to teach" (v. 2) and "manage his own household well" (v. 4). What does that tell us about the role of a pastor? It tells us that the heart of the pastor matters.

Along with the character qualifications, God has also put a gender qualification on who is qualified to serve as a pastor. As you reference back to 1 Timothy 3:1-7 and Titus 1:5-16, you will notice that the gendered pronoun that is used is masculine. The use of the masculine pronoun means that the office of pastor is reserved only for men. Further evidence for the pastorate only being for men is shown through the fact that the New Testament mentions no female pastors. Therefore, to speak of a female pastor is oxymoronic and a defilement of the local church office, which has been given by God.

A final piece of evidence demonstrates that God cares very much about the gender qualifications for the office of pastor is the evidence of context. What I mean by context is the surrounding passage to a particular section of Scripture. For instance, 1 Timothy 3:1-7 has a context to it. In the paragraph just preceding 1 Timothy 3:1-7, Paul instructs women to not function as a pastor. He says, "I do not permit a woman to teach or to exercise authority over a man; rather, she is to remain quiet" (1 Timothy 2:12). Paul mentions two actions that women are not to do in a church over men: teach or exercise authority. These two functions describe broadly the actions of a pastor. The following paragraph in 1 Timothy 3:1-7 shows that Paul had the office of pastor in mind as he wrote these restrictions to women in the church.

I think we need to ask the "why" question to 1 Timothy 2:12. Why does Paul restrict women from the office of pastor? Is Paul being misogynistic by not allowing a women to function as a pastor? To answer the question, we have to look no further than our biblical passage in 1 Timothy 2:13, which says, "For Adam was formed first, then Eve."

Paul answers our "why" question by appealing to a greater authority. Paul appeals to God. He explains that the church is to follow God's order in creation. Essentially, Paul is telling us that the reason women cannot serve as pastor is because God designed male headship to be the function by which His revelation is made known to His people.

A Pastor's Function

A man who meets the character qualifications for the pastorate also has responsibilities that he must fulfill. What we must consider in this section is the function of pastor. You might have an idea already about what a pastor does. For instance, you might think that all a pastor does is preach, teach, visit the sick, and spend time in prayer. Or you might have adopted the view that a pastor is a professional evangelist. It is his job to grow the church. Possibly you view the role of a pastor like the C.E.O. of a business. All these ideas for the function of a pastor are common misunderstandings. The function of a pastor can be described under four simple headings: 1) Leader, 2) Expositor, 3) Shepherd, and 4) Equipper.

A Pastor is a Leader

First, a pastor is a leader. His function is to lead the church. Paul told Timothy that a pastor must be able to "manage" the church (1 Tim. 3:5). Paul uses an interesting term for "manage." The term that Paul uses speaks of a house-manager. This was the word that would have been used to describe the lead servant in a large estate. This servant was responsible for leading all of the other workers in the estate. Many times the house-manager would make financial decisions for the family, educational decisions for the children, and personnel decisions for the staff. The house-manager was essential to the function of the house. Similarly, Paul says that a pastor is to be the "house-manager" of the church. This analogy that Paul makes implies that the pastor is a leader.

A Pastor is an Expositor

Second, a pastor is an expositor of the Word. One of the final charges that Paul gave to a pastor was for Timothy to "preach the Word" (2 Tim. 4:2). The preaching of the Word is essential to the function of a pastor. Biblically faithful pastors preach biblically faithful sermons. The apostles in Jerusalem, who functioned as some of the first pastors, were concerned with neglecting the preaching of the Word so they appointed the forerunners to the office of deacon to handle the daily distribution (Acts 6:2, 4).

A pastor who does not preach the Word commits spiritual neglect upon the church for reasons of malnutrition. The result of not preaching the Word is the scattering of God's people. Jeremiah prophesied, "For the shepherds are stupid and do not *inquire* of the Lord; therefore, they have not prospered, and all their flock is scattered" (Jer. 10:21). A biblical pastor takes preaching seriously.

A Pastor is a Shepherd

Third, a pastor is a shepherd to the sheep. One of the most illustrious metaphors in the Bible to describe the relationship between a pastor and the church is that of a shepherd and sheep. This motif is captured in the definition of the term "pastor," which means shepherd. Jesus, as we know, referred to himself as the "good shepherd" (John 10:11). Likewise, pastors of local churches are to reflect Jesus in their function.

Part of being a shepherd, means that the pastor protects the flock from danger. Paul explains this role of a shepherd in his farewell address to the church in Ephesus. In Acts 20, Paul tells the pastors to guard the flock from "ravenous wolves" that will seek to destroy the church (Acts 20:28-30). This role is inferred from 1 Timothy 1 where Paul is warning the church of the dangers of false teachers, which he refers to as ravenous wolves in Acts 20.

Another aspect of being a shepherd means that the pastor provides for the flock. A great model for understanding the provision that a shepherd gives is found in Psalm 23. The Good Shepherd of Psalm 23 provides green pastures and still waters for the sheep. It is the responsibility of pastors to provide to the church the nutritional value it needs to live a healthy spiritual life. Also, the pastor is to provide the cool waters of the Word to quench the weariness of the soul.

A Pastor is an Equipper

Fourth, a pastor is an equipper of saints and future pastors. In Ephesians 4:11-12, Paul explains that God gave the church pastors for the purpose of equipping "the saints for the work of ministry." The act of being an equipper is rooted in the replication of God's design for disciple-making. In the Great Commission, Jesus commissioned his disciples to make disciples, who in turn would also make disciples. The disciple-making revolution was started by the first pastors of the New Testament church. It is important to note that disciple-making is an action for all believers. However, pastors should set an example before the church to demonstrate the importance of the task.

Not only should pastors be equipping the saints by discipling believers, but they should also be looking to train future pastors. Paul may have had this in mind when he told Timothy, "what you have heard from me in the presence of many witnesses entrust to faithful men who will be *able to teach* others also" (2 Tim. 2:2). It is important that pastors are consistently calling out the called and faithfully equipping those men to be faithful to the Lord in the stewardship of their calling.

Deacon

The second office that God has given to local churches is the office of deacon. The role of a deacon is to serve the church. The pastor leads the church, and the deacon serves the church. This does not mean that the pastor is not a servant, or the deacon is not a leader; instead, the distinction between the two offices comes in how they are recognized in the congregation.

When I became the pastor of First Baptist Church of Immokalee in 2015, the church was in utter disarray. The membership was fractured, the enthusiasm to reach the nations was low, and the leadership structure was non-existent. However, in the midst of all the turmoil, one man stood above the rest and provided spiritual stability. That man was the only deacon in the church. His name is Bill Bethea. His resolve and spiritual acumen served the church in great ways. Much of the revival that the church experienced from 2015 to present can be traced to Bethea's work as a deacon. First Baptist Church of Immokalee would certainly attest to the fact that biblical deacons matter.

The question that we need to consider today is what is it about the role of a deacon that matters to the local church? To answer this question, we will look at three important concepts. First, we will look at the qualifications of a deacon. Second, we will look at the necessity of a deacon. Third, we will look at the ministry of a deacon.

A Deacon's Qualifications

God cares very much about the character of those who occupy the offices of His church. Like we saw with the office of the pastor concerning the qualifications outlined in 1 Timothy 3 and Titus 1, so too God provides certain observable virtues that must be present in a man if he is going to be considered for service as a deacon. These qualifications are found in 1 Timothy 3 and Acts 6. For the sake of brevity, 1 Timothy 3:8-13 will be the passage we will devote attention to for our discussion of a deacon's qualifications. Paul writes to Timothy the following qualifications for a deacon:

> [8] Deacons likewise must be dignified, not double-tongued, not addicted to much wine, not greedy for dishonest gain. [9] They must hold the mystery of the faith with a clear conscience. [10] And let them also be tested first; then let them serve as deacons if they prove themselves blameless. [11] Their wives likewise must be dignified, not slanderers, but sober-minded, faithful in all things. [12] Let deacons each be the husband of one wife, managing their children and their own households well. [13] For those who serve well as deacons gain a good standing for themselves and also great confidence in the faith that is in Christ Jesus.

Like we saw with the office of pastor, God takes seriously the office of deacon. Those who serve in this office must exhibit godliness in their actions; such godliness results in gaining a good standing before Christ Jesus.

A Deacon's Necessity

The purpose of a deacon is birthed out of the needs of a congregation. The launch of the office of deacon came about during a time of evangelistic growth for the early church. Take time and look at Acts 1-6. Notice the amount of growth the church was experiencing. This rapid growth became overwhelming to the local church pastors, resulting in the need for the congregation to call out from among themselves forerunners of the office of deacon. Therefore, the office of deacon is necessitated by the specific needs of a congregation. These needs will be explained in more detail in our next section, "A Deacon's Ministry."

Having qualified men that can meet the needs that come along with a growing church is paramount. At my church, God gave us revival. In 2015, the congregation was hurting. Attendance had plummeted to a depth never experienced in the congregation. Baptisms were infrequent, and spiritual literacy was declining rapidly. However, by the mercies of God, the breath of God's Spirit provided life once again to the church. Baptisms became regular, attendance began to increase, and the church was becoming text-driven in their ministries and mission. The result of the revival produced challenges that I, as their pastor, was unable to fulfill. Thus, in accordance with the precedence set forth in Acts, the congregation set forth a group of men to serve alongside Bill Bethea and me. These men became deacons, and the result of their service is that a congregation, which was on the precipice of death, is now alive and well in southwest Florida.

A Deacon's Ministry

How does a deacon serve in a local church? What are his ministries? To answer these questions, we cannot make a list of specific jobs. However, we can, from biblical passages, deduce overarching ministries that a deacon could be responsible for if the congregation has those specific needs. Therefore, I want to share with you four ways a deacon is called to serve in a local church.

Lead By Example

Deacons can serve by being an example before their local church about what it means to be an active member. New and immature believers need an example set before them of what faithfulness to the Lord looks like in the context of being a member of a local church. I believe this ministry assignment of being an example is implied in the qualifications of 1 Timothy 3. Paul said that deacons should be, "tested first; then let them serve as deacons if they prove themselves blameless" (1 Tim. 3:10). The implication of Paul's statement is that deacons have shown themselves to be an example of godliness before the church, and thus meet the qualifications for being able to serve well as a deacon.

One of the things that I encourage the deacons that serve alongside me is that their ministry first and foremost is to set the example. We want our deacons to demonstrate before the church membership what it looks like to be a faithful church member. We will not consider a deacon to

serve unless they are a "good" church member first. Therefore, we expect our deacons to be active in corporate worship, evangelistic outreaches, and discipleship programs.
This is the minimum of faithfulness that is expected of a
regular church member, so it needs to be the minimum ex-
pectation for a deacon.

Serve the Congregation

Deacons have a responsibility to serve the needs of the
congregation. The forerunner group of men in Acts 6 that
later transitioned into the office of deacon were first tasked
with a practical ministry of service. They were asked to
handle the daily distribution of food and serve tables (Acts
6:2-3). What we learn from Acts 6 is that a deacon's role is
to be a servant to the church. At times, needs arise concerning the care of the congregation that would be a distraction
from the primary responsibilities the Lord has entrusted to
the pastor and His undershepherd. Therefore, it is the deacon's responsibility to serve the pastor and church by meeting those needs of care as they arise.

What type of needs should a deacon meet? Our immediate context of Acts 6 would indicate waiting on tables in
the distribution of food. However, I do not take this passage to be prescriptive, in that deacons can *only* serve tables; instead, this passage needs to be read descriptively. This
means that Luke is describing what occurred in Jerusalem,
and through description we can discern applications from

the passage. Therefore, here is a list of ways that the deacons at Fellowship Church serve the congregation:

- Coordinate the Greeting Team on Sunday and Wednesday
- Collect and count the offering on Sunday
- Communicate regularly with homebound members
- Create volunteer teams for various ministries (children's church, nursery, baptism committee, etc.)
- Clean and prepare the church prior to Sunday and Wednesday

Protect the Peace and Unity

The first century church was not immune to division and discord. The Corinthian congregation was splintered into factions (1 Cor. 1:10-17; 11:17-19). Paul spoke of the doctrinal division that was occurring in Ephesus (1 Tim. 1:3-7). Even in the first congregation of Jerusalem, a dispute arose between members that created disunity (Acts 6:1). The solution for division was for deacons to help protect the peace and unity (Acts 6:3). I want you to notice in Acts 6:5 that the selection of deacons "pleased the whole gathering." A congregation that was once divided because of a dispute between two groups of people has now found unity again because of the role of deacons. Therefore, another ministry of a deacon is to protect peace and unity in their local congregation.

Jesus said in the Sermon on the Mount, "Blessed are the peacemakers, for they shall be called sons of God" (Matt. 5:9). All believers have a responsibility "to guard the unity of the Spirit in the bond of peace" (Eph. 5:3). However, I believe that deacons have been given a particular responsibility to be an example in this area of ministry.

How can a deacon practically protect the peace and unity of the church? First, by virtue of their office, members will seek their advice. It is important for a deacon to respond biblically in his advice. Giving counsel that is void of biblical truth is breeding ground for disunity and division. Second, deacons protect the peace and unity of a congregation through being watchful. In Acts 6, a group of widows in the church were being neglected. You could say that these neglected widows were being overlooked. Therefore, a deacon's role is to be watchful in the congregation. Watchfulness occurs through seeking to befriend someone sitting alone, looking around the congregation for families that might need a little extra help with their children, or praying with a person as they share a need. All of these examples will contribute to peace and unity in a local church.

Support the Pastors

The final ministry of a deacon is to support the pastors. This support is not to come blindly, but instead it is a support of the pastor's ministry. In Acts 6, these forerunners of deacons served in such a manner that supported their pastors. This support allowed for the pastors to devote more attention to the ministries of preaching and praying. Having deacons that serve faithfully is an invaluable blessing to a pastor and congregation. Here are some ways that a deacon can support His pastor:

- Pray with the pastor before the Worship Service.
- Help his wife care for His kids on Sunday morning.
- Speak positively about the mission and vision of the church.
- Do not bring attention to yourself, but rather point the church to Jesus.
- Offer to assist in member care (i.e. visitation, hospital visits, etc.)

Conclusion

God has given to His church two offices: pastors and deacons. These offices assist in the maturity of the body of Christ. God has given clear qualifications for each office. In these qualifications, we learn who can serve, how they are to serve, and what their service entails. The fact that such attention is given by God to the qualifications indicates that the local church matters to Him and it should still matter to us.

Discussion Questions:

1. What authority does a pastor have with a congregation?

2. Read Psalm 23 and share how Jesus's shepherding relates to the function of a pastor?

3. Which function of a pastor do you see happening less in churches? Why?

4. Which ministry of a deacon do you see functioning least in churches? Why?

Chapter 6

The Polity of the Church:
A Biblical Case for Congregational Polity

*"And let us consider how to stir up one another to love and good works,
not neglecting to meet together, as is the habit of some, but encouraging
one another, and all the more as you see the Day drawing near."*
Hebrews 10:24-25

Are Southern Baptist churches functioning according to the polity outlined in the New Testament? According to an article by Dwayne Hastings, Southern Baptists have a skewed understanding of what it means to adhere to congregational polity. Hastings, in his article, addressed the distortions of congregational polity that are prevalent in Southern Baptist churches. Essentially, Hastings reports that thousands of Southern Baptist churches are governed by the proxy of a deacon board. What is alarming about this article is that Hastings points out that these churches, which concede governance to the deacons, are still operating under the assumption that they are congregational. He explains the board of deacons is "exercising great authority in the midst of congregational rule."[22] Such divergence from authentic congregational governance, which is outlined in the New Testament, contributes, as Hastings contends, to the decline of church attendance. Hastings quoted Talbot School of Theology professor, Gary L. MacIntosh, to say the deacon governed model, "ensures the church will not grow."[23] The question arises, "At what point did Southern Baptist churches go astray in their adherence to congregational governance?"

Several prominent Southern Baptists have issued their response to this question. James Sheffield concludes that Southern Baptists have relied too much on their traditions without adequately looking to the Scriptures. He said, "The Scriptures are to inform our tradition, not our traditions interpreting Scripture for us."[24] Paige Patterson concurs with Sheffield's remarks, but goes a step further by stating that Southern Baptists have emphasized personal autonomy to such an extent that the Holy Spirit is non-existent. He said, "I fear that what we have created in our Baptist churches is a fierce individualism that is so autonomous that it is autonomy from the Holy Spirit."[25] James Merritt, in the same article, addresses the root cause for why Southern Baptist churches have governed themselves outside the biblical parameters of congregationalism. Merritt says the cause can be traced to, "there being too much world in the church and not enough church in the world."[26]

If Hastings' article is any indication of a serious distortion of congregational polity in Southern Baptist churches, then there is a great need for a recovery of the New Testament teaching of congregational polity. This chapter seeks to argue that congregational governance matters because it is God's prescribed polity according to the practices in the book of Acts. This chapter will have two major headings. First, a brief outline of the alternative ecclesiastical systems that one might encounter in churches. Second, three case studies from Acts will serve as the biblical foundation for the New Testament practice of congregational governance. Each case study will show an aspect of the church's function.

SURVEY OF ECCLESIASTICAL SYSTEMS

Baptists, Methodists, and Catholics would each refer to their denomination and churches as being Christian; however, similarities end immediately when one begins to describe how these churches are governed. Church governance seeks to answer the question, "Who rules the church?"[27] At times, church government is referred to as polity. The word polity, as Sullivan has said, "is a system by which a group of people choose to govern themselves or are governed."[28] Sullivan would later explain, the crux of polity is the understanding of authority, and it is upon one's understanding of who holds authority that defines the "basis by which they will relate."[29]

The traditional approach to speaking about church governance is to divide the discussion into three categories: Episcopalianism, Presbyterianism, and Congregationalism. James Leo Garrett, former professor at Southwestern Baptist Theological Seminary, referenced several Baptist authors who have classified church polity by the three proposed monikers.[30] However, Garrett adds a fourth category to the three traditional approaches. He refers to this fourth approach as "Papal Polity."[31] Gerald Cowen, formerly at Criswell College and Southeastern Baptist Theological Seminary, echoes Garrett's work when he said, "There are three basic approaches to church government."[32] James Sullivan classified church polity by examining the structure of denominations. He expanded the traditional three classifications to six classifications that were prevalent during his time of writing.[33]

Baptists are not the only ones who have adopted the three traditional classifications for describing church polity. Steven Cowan's edited book, *Who Runs the Church? Four Views on Church Government* provided provocative discourse between the various ecclesiastical leaders concerning their viewpoints of church government. He uses the three headings, but splits congregationalism into two categories, which constitutes the four views that he evaluated.[34] Erickson's *Christian Theology* has the traditional three classifications, but concludes with a final classification, which he calls "non-governmental."[35]

Though there are some variations as to there being three or four classifications, it has been demonstrated that there is unity within the three major classifications of Episcopalianism, Presbyterianism, and Congregationalism. Therefore, the goal of this section is to give a fair introductory explanation of the three broad classifications for church polity. Then in subsequent sections show how Congregationalism is the church government structure of the New Testament, particularly in Acts.

Episcopalianism

The first church government that is to be explained is Episcopalianism. This term was used by Peter Toon in his chapter in the book, *Who Runs the Church?* Toon defined Episcopalianism.

> Those churches which maintain the historical episcopate claim that their polity is based upon that which developed in the providential guidance of God from the apostolic age through the first few centuries of the Christian church. For them, this means that it is both wholly in accord with apostolic teaching and takes into account the practical result of the evangelization, church planting, and teaching of the apostles, their fellow workers, and their successors.[36]

Therefore, it is essential for Toon to establish the biblical usage of the term "bishop" because he claims it is that term which unites all who adhere to Episcopalianism.[37] Garrett, likewise, sympathizes with Toon's desire to demonstrate "bishop" as being used to communicate church polity in the New Testament. Garrett explained in volume 1 of his systematic theology,

> Appeal is made in support of episcopal polity to the fact that Paul and Barnabas toward the end of the first mission journey 'appointed' 'elders' for the believers 'in each church' (Acts 14:23), to the leadership role exercised by James in the church in Jerusalem (Acts 15:13), and to Paul's instruction to Titus to 'appoint elders in every town' in Crete (Tit. 1:5).[38]

Episcopalianism emphasizes the oversight function of the bishop towards the congregation.

The authority within Episcopalianism rest with the bishops because they are unbroken successors to the apostles.[39] They function as the leader of the church in every facet as it applies to the church fulfilling the mission of the Kingdom. Garret outlined the authoritative function of the bishops in Episcopalianism. He said, "Among the duties normally exercised by bishops are the ordination of priests (or elders), the placement of priests (or elders) in pastoral assignments, the confirmation of the baptized, the preservation and teaching of true doctrine, and the exercise of discipline."[40] The authority of the church lies in the bishops. Therefore, according to the Episcopalians, bishops matter.

Presbyterianism

The second church government classification that is tradi-
tionally recognized is Presbyterianism. Erickson notes that
Presbyterianism focuses on a particular office within the
church just like Episcopalianism.[41] Presbyterian government, according to Harris, emphasizes the role and office
of the elder (presbyter).[42] Erickson noted that Presbyterianism, which emphasizes the role of the elder, has a history in
the Jewish Synagogue.[43] The ruling nature of elders in the
church is on a delegate basis. Taylor agrees with Erickson
that Presbyterianism as a governance is found throughout
the Old and New Testament.[44] According to Taylor, the
church exists within both Testaments, and he provides four
conclusions for his assertions. He says:

> (1) They have the same Savior—the Lord Jesus Christ;
> (2) they have the same destiny—heaven; (3) they are
> saved on the same basis—the grace of God, and (4) they
> receive eternal life by the same instrumentality—faith.
> Therefore, Presbyterian ecclesiology (theology of the
> church) prefers the term "biblical church," not just the
> "New Testament church."

Because of the continuity between the Testaments,
churches do not function, according to Taylor, "independent, but interdependent."[45]

The interdependence of local churches extends beyond
cooperation and is foundational to Presbyterian governance.

The organizational structure that maintains this interdependence is outlined by Erickson. He explains,

> All the churches in one area are governed by the presbytery (Presbyterian) or classis (Reformed), which is made up of one lay elder and one minister from each consistory (Reformed) or one lay elder from each session and all the ministers in the area (Presbyterian). The next grouping is the synod, made up of an equal number of lay elders and clergy chosen by each presbytery or classis. At the highest level the Presbyterian Church also has a General Assembly, composed again of lay and clergy representatives from the presbyteries.[46]

This ecclesiastical structure places the authority outside of the local congregation and into the hierarchy of elders. Pendleton noted in his book, *Baptist Church Manual*, that any appeal to the General Assembly would be, "final and irresistible;" thus, making the authority of the local congregation non-existent.[47] Erickson concludes, "It is at the level of the elders that divine authority actually functions within the church."[48] Therefore, according to Presbyterianism, elders matter.

Congregationalism

The previous two forms of church government focused on offices within the church. For instance, Episcopalianism focused on the role and office of the bishop and Presbyterianism focused on the role and office of the elder. The third major ecclesiastical structure is Congregationalism. Proponents of Congregationalism include Baptists and other free church tradition churches.[49]

Defining and explaining Congregationalism within Baptist ecclesiology must begin with identifying the parameters for the discussion. Unlike those who adhere to Presbyterianism and Episcopalianism, those who hold to Congregationalism utilize one source for their authority, the New Testament.[50] Baptist theologian, R. Stanton Norman wrote in his book, *The Baptist Way*, "Baptists have contended that the New Testament has established the manner in which a local church is to govern and administrate itself."[51] J. L. Dagg explained in his book, *Manual of Church Order*, that churches should govern themselves after the examples set by the apostles.[52] W. T. Connor concurs with Dagg and Norman about the New Testament being the source for Congregationalism. He says, "Several reasons might be given why the church should be organized in a democratic manner. First, the New Testament churches were organized on this plan."[53] Therefore, the New Testament sets the parameters for Congregationalism.

Baptists draw several conclusions from the New Testament as it pertains to church governance. First, Baptists conclude that Christ is the ultimate head of the church. Patterson notes that any discussion pertaining to church polity is, "doomed from the outset unless it begins with Christ, the head of the church."[54] The notion of Christ's supremacy in the church manifests itself through a service-oriented mission. Congregants and leadership are both servants then of the same master, Jesus Christ. Edmund Clowney noted in his book, *The Church,* "The church is not like the kingdoms of this world, for it is organized for service, not dominion. All government in the church is stewardship: i.e. its leaders are servant-managers, who use their authority only to advance the interest of those they represent and serve."[55] Therefore, the leader of the church is Christ, and He has entrusted that leadership to the local members of His body, the church.

Second, Baptists conclude from the New Testament that Congregationalism places an emphasis on the liberty (autonomy) and equality (priesthood) of the individual believers as he relates to the Lordship of Christ. Allen addresses individual autonomy and equality in his chapter in the book *Upon This Rock.* He says, "At the center of Baptist ecclesiology is the notion of the believers' church. The concept of autonomy is vital to Baptist theology and is in fact part of the warp and woof of what it means to be Baptist.[56] Garrett explains that Congregationalism functions through democratic process. He says, "Such congregationalism means internally the affirmation that every member of the congregation has 'a voice in its affairs and its decisions.'"[57] The democratic process is functionally inept, but a necessity. According to Norman H. Maring and Winthrop S. Hudson, [Christ intended] the full participation of the members of the church in its total life, as implied in the doctrine of the priesthood of all believers."[58]

The third conclusion Baptists arrive at as it pertains to the New Testament understanding of Congregationalism is that the church has two offices, pastor and deacon.[59] The offices of pastor and deacon are, in essence, equal to the laity, but functionally they are different in their service to the laity under the Lordship of Christ. Pastor's functionally fulfill the threefold office of shepherd, bishop, and elder.[60] The function of the deacon is to be servant or assistant.[61] Pendleton applied the predicament recorded in Acts 6 to conclude the following about the office of the deacon, "Thus the creation of the office of deacon recognizes the fact that the duties of pastors are preeminently spiritual; and that they should not be overburdened with other interests of the churches."[62] Therefore, deacons are a gift to the pastor through attending to physical matters of the local church. They, like the pastors, are equal to the laity because of the sufficiency of the atonement and the Lordship of Christ.

EXAMPLES OF CONGREGATIONAL POLITY IN ACTS

If Congregationalism is espoused as being the governmental polity of local churches in the New Testament, then what case studies are there in the New Testament to support the assumptions outlined in the argumentation section for Congregationalism? Three case studies will be examined from Acts as examples that Congregationalism was the mode of church governance in the New Testament.[63] The three passages that will serve as case studies were selected for two reasons. One, each passage occurs during a different time in the book, which demonstrates that congregationalism was a regular practice in the early church. Two, the passages show Congregationalism from two separate churches. This confirms the normality of Congregationalism among the early church.

Acts 6:
Election of Servants

The first example of Congregationalism recorded in Acts involves the election of servants to adhere to the serious problem of neglect concerning the distribution of goods. The widows that were Hellenistic were being overlooked by the Hebraic Jews as it pertained to the, "daily distribution" (Acts 6:1). This problem arose, according to Polhill, as a result of the rapid expansion of the church. Polhill says, "The Jerusalem Christian community had witnessed considerable growth; and as is so often the case with rapid increase, administrative problems developed."[64] According to Norman, this administrative problem proposed two questions: first, "how would the daily distribution of food take place, and [second], who would be responsible for this task?"[65] The answer to these two questions come about in the Jerusalem congregation through the workings of congregationalism.

Congregationalism was demonstrated in Acts 6 by the subservient leadership of the apostles (Acts 6:2-4). The apostles recognized the problem and led through democratic process. First, upon recognizing the problem, they, "summoned the full number of disciples" (Acts 6:2). Even though the dispute impacted only a portion of the congregation, the apostles saw the need for the entire congregation to participate in the solution. Second, the apostles demonstrated pastoral leadership by directing the congregation to the proper steps which needed to be taken to resolve the conflict (Acts 6:3). The apostles did not exercise their leadership in a dictating manner, but rather allowed the congregation to, "pick out from among" themselves men, which corresponded to a carefully outlined biblical standard of character (Acts 6:3).

Congregationalism was also demonstrated through the governance of the congregation. The problem of physical neglect concerning the Hellenistic Jews was a congregational problem, and thus the solution needed to be addressed by the congregation. Norman astutely remarks, "Although the apostles were present, the manner in which the issue was addressed and resolved was congregational. The apostles looked to the church to assume ownership of this issue and resolve the problem. The entire congregation had the responsibility to identify those who were qualified to perform this ministry."[66] Even though the congregation was guided by the leadership of the apostles, it was ultimately the congregation that was "pleased" with the approach of the apostles (Acts 6:4). The concept of "pleased" denotes a response that shows the humility of the congregation to meet the needs of the people and a respect for the one offering the advice.[67] Therefore, the congregation held the authority to approve or disapprove the proposed solution by the apostles, but because the proposed solution was presented in such a manner that affirmed congregational polity and they respected the authority of the apostles, who were functioning as their pastors, the congregation voted in favor.

The consequence of congregational polity, when it is done according to Scripture is outlined in Acts 6 as being very positive. One commentator remarked, "Positive results came almost immediately from the wise and effective handling of the Grecians' complaint."[68] The first consequence was that the church had unity and protected peace among the body. Bence notes, "The church, in unity and the power of the Spirit, continued to move forward in rapid growth."[69] The second consequence of congregational polity is that the church will, through their unity, advance the Great Commission. The text illustrates the advancement of the Great Commission through two phrases. One, "the word of God continued to increase" and two, "and the number of disciples multiplied greatly in Jerusalem" (Acts 6:7). The first phrase explains the growth of God's Word. Peterson described the growth of God's word in these terms,

> The satisfactory resolution of the conflict in the Jerusalem church made it possible for this ministry of the gospel to flourish and for church growth to take place even more *rapidly (sphodra)*. Church growth continued because the word of God had free course among the believers, and outsiders were able to witness its practical effect in a loving, united community, as well as hear its challenge from the lips of the apostles.[70]

The second phrase shows that when the Word of God grows the natural fruit which comes forth is a disciple. A disciple cannot be made without the implanted Word of God. These two consequences are a direct result of a local church governing congregationally.

Acts 13:
Commissioning of Missionaries

A second example of congregational polity comes in Acts 13:1-3 with the commissioning of missionaries to serve. Acts 13 is the account of Paul and Barnabas being commissioned on their first missionary journey, a journey that would take them as missionaries to the Gentiles. It was in the midst of the exhortation of the prophets and teachers during congregational worship that the entire congregation was impressed by the Holy Spirit to commission Paul and Barnabas as missionaries.

Congregationalism is supported by two key aspects in the text. First, Congregationalism is seen through the Holy Spirit's speech. Norman contends, "that the Holy Spirit's instructions were directed to the entire church at Antioch."[71] Lange agrees with Norman that the Spirit was addressing the entire church when he said, "Luke proceeds to describe the directions which the Spirit gave to the Church respecting the appointment of Barnabas and Saul as missionaries."[72] Lange comes to this conclusion of Congregationalism because of the use of αυτων in verse 2. Lange says αυτων, "is not addressed solely to the teachers, but rather to the whole congregation."[73] Second, Congregationalism is seen through the church's response to the command of the Spirit. The text explains that the church, collectively, laid their hands on Paul and Barnabas and "sent them off" (Acts 13:3). Just as the Spirit spoke to the entire congregation, the entire congregation acted in agreement as they commissioned Paul and Barnabas.

The consequence that arises from Congregational polity in the church of Antioch is the expansion of the Great Commission. The immediate context describes Paul and Barnabas's ministry as preaching the Word of God throughout the, "whole island as far as Paphos" (Acts 13:5-6). Later in Acts 13, Paul and Barnabas's ministry is described as reaching an entire city (Acts 13:44). Therefore, it appears from the immediate context that Congregationalism fuels Great Commission ministry.

Acts 15:
Settling of Doctrinal Disputes

The churches of Antioch and Jerusalem continued to govern themselves by congregational polity. In Acts 15, Congregationalism is demonstrated through a doctrinal dispute between the church of Antioch and the church of Jerusalem.[74] The way these churches addressed the doctrinal dispute demonstrated their adherence to congregational polity. Daniel Akin references six examples from Acts 15 of how congregational polity was used to resolve the problem.[75]

First, a committee was formed by the church of Antioch to go and address the dispute in Jerusalem (Acts 15:2). Luke uses the phrase, "sent on their way by the church" to demarcate that the decision of who to send to Jerusalem was a congregational decision. Furthermore, the committee from Antioch was received by the church in Jerusalem. Acts 15:4 says, "they were welcomed by the church." Just in the opening verses, it is clear that the congregations are heavily involved in the discussion." The congregation decided but in context James led, others contributed to the discussion, James offered a solution, and the church decided on the solution and sent the letter to the church of Antioch. In summary, it seems to me that James (likely the half-brother of Jesus) was serving as the Pastor at FBC Jerusalem, the Apostles and other elders contributed, and the congregation decided.

Second, Acts 15 demonstrates congregational polity because, as Akin states, "the church initiated the activity, not the apostles or other leaders."[76] Luke makes it clear that the church initiated the activity by saying that, "Paul and Barnabas and some others were appointed to go up to Jerusalem" (Acts 15:2). Their appointment, as already explained in Acts 15:3, was a decision of the congregation. Therefore, it was not the decision of the apostles or elders to bring resolution to the dispute, but the congregation governing according to their biblical mandates.

Third, the entire congregation in Jerusalem was part of the discussion concerning the theological teaching that was brought to Antioch from Jerusalem. Acts 15:12 indicates that the entire congregation was present for the discussion, but due to the nature of the conversation they allowed the apostles and elders to "consider the matter" (Acts 15:6). This decision by the congregation affirms pastoral leadership without denying congregational polity. The Jerusalem church saw it necessary to give the matter to their spiritual leaders (apostles and elders), and remained engaged through a silent presence.

Fourth, the Jerusalem church decided as a congregation to send representatives to Antioch to bring reconciliation in a cooperative manner to the two churches. Acts 15:22 explains that it was agreeable to the apostles, elders, and church to send these representatives to Antioch.

Fifth, the letter, that was composed by the apostles and elders in Jerusalem and approved by the Jerusalem congregation, was sent by a chosen representative committee to the whole congregation in Antioch (Acts 15:23).

Sixth, not only was the intent of the letter to be given to the entire congregation, but when it was delivered the entire congregation received the letter.

Pastoral leadership, local church autonomy, like-minded cooperation, and democratic process were all shown through these six examples of congregational polity. Like the previous examples from Acts 6 and 13, the consequences of congregational polity are Great Commission advancement and unity among the church. The unity is described by the manner in which the congregation received the letter from the Jerusalem church, as described in Acts 15:31-34. Furthermore, the Great Commission advanced as a result.

Paul and Barnabas were now able to focus on preaching and teaching the Word (Acts 15:35).

CONCLUSION

Is Congregationalism the biblical norm for church polity in the New Testament? Through a survey of the other ecclesiastical structures and a theological examination of Congregationalism as a system, it would appear that Congregationalism is biblical. Furthermore, the three case studies from Acts validated not only its biblical precedence, but also its biblical norm in the life of the early local churches. Three significant events in the life of the early church proved that Congregationalism was the preferred biblical method for church polity. The fruit that came from churches which practiced Congregationalism was Great Commission advancement and unity among the congregation. Therefore, it has been demonstrated that Congregationalism is the intended practice of church governance in the New Testament. Because the local church matters, how a local church is governed also matters. Therefore, congregational polity matters.

DISCUSSION QUESTIONS:

1. What has been your experience with church polity? Which of the three major categories (Episcopalian-

ism, Presbyterianism, and Congregationalism) have you seen practiced?

2. What do you think is the difference between a congregation governing and a congregation leading?

3. What does congregational polity reveal about the importance of every believer in a church?

4. What are some potential struggles that a congregational church could face?

Chapter 7

The Mission of the Church:
Go and Make Disciples

"And Jesus came and said to them, 'All authority in heaven and on earth has been given to me. Go therefore and make disciples of all nations, baptizing them in the name of the Father and of the Son and of the Holy Spirit, teaching them to observe all that I have commanded you. And behold, I am with you always, to the end of the age.'"
Matthew 28:18-20

"so that through the church the manifold wisdom of God might now be made known to the rulers and authorities in the heavenly places."
Ephesians 3:10

L et me ask you some questions—Why does it matter that Jesus is the foundation of the church? Why does it matter that a church recognizes only those who are regenerate as members? Why does baptism matter? Why does the Lord's Supper matter? Why do deacons matter? Why do pastors matter? Finally, why does it matter that a church be governed by the congregation? Why do any of these questions matter? Ultimately, why does the local church matter?

The answer to the question, why does the local church matter, lies within God's ultimate mission for the church. The local church matters because the Great Commission matters. God's extraordinary plan for the evangelization and discipleship of the world is through the ordinary means of local churches being about the Great Commission.

Churches today have more programs and methods than at any other point in history. The church growth world has provided pastors with a myriad of gadgets and gizmos to bolster attendance, increase budget, and "reach" their communities with the "gospel." However, in the midst of all of the promises made by the gurus of church growth, there is still a tried and true method outlined in the New Testament for what the sole purpose of a local church should be about. That "tried and true" method is the Great Commission.

I will never forget preaching through the book of Acts and arriving at Acts 17:6. In this passage, Luke describes how the church was being credited with having "turned the world upside down" with the message of the gospel (Acts 17:6). Pondering on that phrase, I began to meditate upon how a small group of uneducated fishermen could be accredited with making the gospel known to such an extent that the world looked differently because of their ministry.

As I meditated upon Acts 17:6, I realized the key to the success of those men. Their success was not because they had a fun children's ministry. Their success was not because they had an engaging student ministry, or because their music was relevant. Their success was not because their preaching appeased the ear of those in the churches. Instead, the success that the church experienced in the first century was the outworking of the Holy Spirit upon a group of people that sought to make the Great Commission their only mission. The first century church understood that the local church mattered; therefore, the Great Commission matters.

In this chapter, I want to awaken your mind to the prospect that the *only* mission of the church is the Great Commission. To accomplish this goal, we will spend most of our time in Matthew 28:18-20. We will consider several headings. First, we will look at the power of the Great Commission. Second, we will look at the purpose of the Great Commission. Finally, we will consider the promise of the Great Commission.

THE POWER OF
THE GREAT COMMISSION

First, I want us to consider the *power* of the Great Commission. In and of ourselves, we are powerless. Scripture teaches in John 15 that apart from the work of Jesus through us, we can do nothing (John 15:5). Any good that a church does in reference to the Great Commission comes from the empowerment of God. God's power is explained in the Great Commission through Jesus's pronouncement in verse 18, where he said, "All authority in heaven and on earth has been given to me." Jesus declaring that He possesses all authority is a statement of His triumph over sin and death. He is proving his power and sovereignty.

The power of God is accessible to the church through the authoritative gospel-message that the church proclaims. Jesus explained to His disciples that they had the authoritative power of the keys of God's Kingdom (Matt. 16:19). These keys of the gospel message can unlock the prison bars of sin and the shackles of death which enslave every person who is not a believer. As a church, we have been commissioned by God, under His authority to make known this glorious gospel message that can change lives forever.

THE PURPOSE OF THE GREAT COMMISSION

Second, I want us to consider the *purpose* of the Great Commission. In Matthew 28:18-20, the main verb upon which the door of the entire commission hinges is the verb "make disciples." The purpose of the Great Commission is not evangelization, though that is important. The purpose of the Great Commission is disciple-making. The term "disciple" was used among the Greeks as a word to describe an apprentice. This apprentice would learn closely from the teacher his philosophical worldview. In application for the church, new believers are to be in an apprentice relationship with a more mature believer and learn from instruction the way that the Bible teaches how one should view the world.

One of the clearest examples of disciple-making in the New Testament, outside of the ministry of Jesus with the original twelve disciples, is the discipleship relationship between Paul and Timothy. Paul instructs Timothy as a father would a son (1 Tim. 1:2; 2 Tim. 2:1). His admonition to Timothy to pass on the doctrine that he has heard to "faithful men who will be able to teach others also" is an example of the multiplication of discipleship (2 Tim. 2:2). Disciples are made when they are making disciples.

The question you might be wondering is, what process do I use to make disciples? Is there a secret, ironclad formula that is tried and true that will result in a disciple who makes disciples? These are valid questions, and I would direct your attention back to our Great Commission passage in Matthew 28. Jesus surrounds the main verb—"make disciples"—with three participles, which function with the imperatival force of the main verb they modify.

Going After the Lost With Conviction

Matthew 28:19 begins with the actionable command for disciples to be going. Disciples are made when they are going after the lost with conviction. From the beginning of Jesus's ministry until His ascension, we see that Jesus was concerned about the eternal state of humanity. From His first sermon recorded in Mark 1:14 all the way to His last statements in Acts 1:8, we see that Jesus is concerned about the lost hearing the good news of the gospel. Luke's Gospel even states that Jesus's purpose was to "seek and save those who are lost" (Lk 19:10). Therefore, as students of the master teacher, Jesus, it is our responsibility to have as one of our core convictions to go after those who are lost without Christ.

Connecting Believers in a Local Church

Not only is disciple-making about training a new believer to be going after the lost with conviction; it is also about connecting new believers to a local church. Jesus explains that disciple-making involves baptizing. The purpose for baptism is for believers to express outwardly their identification with Christ. This outward expression is administered in conjunction with a local church. Evidence of support for baptism being a local church ordinance is found in Acts 2. Scripture teaches that those who repented of their sins were then baptized and added to the church (Acts 2:47).

Being connected to a local church is crucial in the disciple-making process. It is through a local church that a disciple grows and matures as a believer. Paul, writing to the Ephesians, explains that through the church a believer matures into the "stature of the fullness of Christ" (Eph. 4:12-13). This process of maturation for the believer is inaugurated by the ordinance of baptism. Baptism is the first act of obedience that sets off the chain reaction of continual obedience to God through the teaching of the Word.

Teaching About the Love of Christ

The final essential element of God's plan for disciple-making is teaching believers about the love of Christ. Disciple-making is more than evangelism and church membership. Disciple-making is training a believer to be a teacher of God's Word, who then makes disciples.

Now, it is true that some people are gifted in the area of teaching. God has set apart a particular office in His church for teaching—office of pastor. However, teaching is not just a pastoral responsibility. Instead, teaching is a responsibility of all believers. It is the responsibility of every Christian to be teaching the Word of God through the means of disciple-making.

A clear example of the teaching responsibility for every believer is seen through the responsibility of parents in Deuteronomy 6. Parents are commanded by God to teach their children the Law of God. This act of teaching was a precursor to God's design of disciple-making because parents were instructed to teach their children formally at home and informally in the gates (Deut. 6:4-9). Likewise, spiritual parents, those who have led a person to new birth by the Spirit, are responsible for teaching their spiritual children the Word of God.

The command in Matthew 28:20 is for a disciple to be teaching all that Jesus has commanded. This includes the entirety of Scripture. Genesis to Revelation is the textbook of disciple-making. One of the best practices a disciple can do for the process of making disciples is to teach a believer how to read and study the Word of God. We need to be teaching young believers to read the Bible, rely on the Holy Spirit, interpret the passage in context, and apply the Word to their life. Let me challenge you to incorporate the basic principles of Bible study into your disciple-making. If you are unfamiliar with how to study the Bible, then here are several steps you can take to begin the process of studying your Bible:

- Step 1: Pray and ask God to give you wisdom and knowledge as you study.
- Step 2: Read a chapter at a time through a book of the Bible.
- Step 3: Write down a summary of what you read.
- Step 4: Ask the question, what does this passage mean?
- Step 5: Ask the question, how do I apply the meaning to my life?

Though these five-steps are not exhaustive, they will help you to cultivate a life habit of Bible study that the Lord will use to sanctify you with His truth (John 17:17).

THE PROMISE OF
THE GREAT COMMISSION

So far, we have looked at the *power* of the Great Commission and the *purpose* of the Great Commission. Finally, I want us to consider the *promise* of the Great Commission. Certainly, the task of making disciples of *all nations* is a daunting exploration for anyone to embark upon. There should be a sense of weight pressing down on your shoulders from the responsibility that God has assigned to us as believers.

While the weight of making disciples is great, we must not forget what Jesus said when He told His disciples that His "yoke is easy and his burden is light" (Matt. 11:30). God in His goodness did not leave us abandoned in this great task of disciple-making. He has provided us with a glorious promise—His presence. Jesus assures His disciples that He will be with them always (Matt. 28:20). The promise of the presence of God for the task of disciple-making is reassuring because then we know that God will complete the tasks that He has set forth.

One of the most encouraging verses to me in the New Testament is 1 Thessalonians 5:24, which says, "He who calls you is faithful; He will surely do it." I find great encouragement in knowing that God will do it. Paul told the Philippians that the work that God began in them will be completed (Phil. 1:6).

The task of making disciples is the mission of the church. God has chosen for His people under His authority to, "Go and make disciples of all nations, baptizing them in the name of the Father and of the Son and of the Holy Spirit, teaching them to observe all that I have commanded you" (Matt. 28:19-20). Such a task is weighty, but "to whom much is given, of him much will be required" (Lk 12:48).

Therefore, the local church matters because the Great Commission matters!

Discussion Questions:

1. What is the biggest fear you have in disciple-making?

2. How does the fact that making disciples is a command from Jesus change your urgency to participate in the Great Commission?

3. In your own words, what is the mission of a local church?

4. How can social and mercy ministries detract from the core mission of a local church?

Chapter 8

Conclusion

Does the local church still matter? I think we can say confidently that the local church does still matter. God in His infinite knowledge particularly chose the church to be His program for the execution of the Great Commission among His followers. As Ronnie Rogers said in his chapter of *Does It Still Matter?*, "The local church is at the heart of Christ's plan to build the universal church."[77] You cannot read Matthew 28:18-20 without understanding Ephesians 4:11-12. These two passages go together and help to show why the local church still matters today.

If the local church does still matter, then I think the question becomes what happens next. What should you and I do with the truth that God has designed and planned for local churches to be the vehicle that takes the gospel to the nations? I want to offer several practical action steps you need to take concerning the knowledge you have learned about the local church.

BECOME A MEMBER OF A LOCAL CHURCH

The first action step that you need to take is to become a member of a local church. Joining a church is a big commitment. However, God has a designed function for you in the context of a local church to exercise the gifts that He has provided you. Failure to use your gifts within a local covenant body of other baptized believers would not be good stewardship of His grace-gifts to you.

In choosing a local church to join, it is important that you keep in mind what you have learned. Remember, you are not looking to join a perfect church. Such a church does not exist. However, you are looking to join a church that practices the principles that the New Testament outlines for a healthy church. For instance, you want to find a church that has Jesus as the foundation, regenerate church membership as its constitution, baptism and Lord's Supper as its ordinances, qualified pastors and deacons as its officers, congregationalism as its governance, and the Great Commission as its mission. These are the pillar principles of what the New Testament teaches for recognizing what is and what is not a legitimate local church.

BE A GIVING MEMBER OF
A LOCAL CHURCH

Once you have joined a local church, it is important that you become part of the life of the church. Make sure that you are contributing to the spiritual health of the congregation. I like to think of church members contributing to the health of a church through them being a giving member. By giving, what I mean is that a church member gives of their time, talents, and treasures.

A simple way to be a good member of a local church is through faithfulness; this is the giving of your time. As a pastor, I can attest that one of the most frustrating aspects of church members is the inconsistency they practice with their attendance. By simply making the Sunday gathering a priority for your family, you will immediately be contributing to the health of the congregation.

Also, you can contribute to the health of a local church by asking how you can serve; this is the giving of your talents. Oftentimes, pastors and ministry leaders are searching tirelessly to find helpers for their respective ministries. By making yourself available to serve in any way your church needs, you will immediately be contributing to your church's health. One area that always needs help is children's ministry. Go there first and ask if you can help in the nursery. I promise, you will be a wonderful help.

The final way that you can contribute to the health of a local church is through being faithful with your tithes and offerings; this is giving your treasures. The New Testament talks about how the Lord loves a cheerful giver (2 Cor. 9:6-11). Being a cheerful giver at your church will help to support your pastoral leadership and the taking of the gospel to the nations.

Be a Going Member of a Local Church

Joining a church is important. Giving your time, talents, and treasures is important. The final practical action that you can do is to be a going member of a local church. What do I mean? I mean that you are actively sharing the gospel and seeking to grow the Kingdom of God through being a faithful witness. As a pastor, the most encouraging messages that I receive from church members is when they share with me about how they are making disciples. Knowing that my congregation is living a life that is on mission for Jesus is the best encouragement. I am sure that your pastor will be encouraged when you share with him that you are making Jesus known to your friends, family, and neighbors.

My prayer is that you will take what you have learned in these chapters, and you will serve our Lord through one of His local churches, because the local church still matters!

Endnotes

1. 1 C.S. Lewis. *Screwtape Letters*, 5.

2. Ibid., 5

3. The six behaviors that Thom Rainer outlined in his article, "Why Dying Churches Die" are: 1) They refuse to admit they are sick, very sick, 2) They are still waiting on the "magic bullet" pastor, 3) They fail to accept responsibility, 4) They are not willing to change…at all, 5) Their "solutions" are inwardly focused, 6) They desire to return to 1985. (https://thomrainer.com/2017/08/dying-churches-die/).

4. Daniel L. Akin. *Theology for the Church* (Nashville, TN: B&H Publishing Group, 2014), 406.

5. Ibid, 408.

6. Ibid.

7. J.L. Reynolds, Church Polity. The Baptist Distinctives Series: Number 25. (Paris, AR: The Baptist Standard Bearer, Inc., 2006), 56.

8. Malcom Yarnell, *Upon This Rock*. (Nashville, TN: B&H Publishing Group, 2010), 30.

9. John Nolland, *The Gospel of Matthew: A Commentary on the Greek Text, New International Greek Testament Commentary* (Grand Rapids, MI; Carlisle: W.B. Eerdmans; Paternoster Press, 2005), 747. It is important to note that Nolland believes that Matthew's usage of the term "church" is to reference a restored Israel. This thought denies the notion that the church is a new institution. The researcher does not hold to the position of replacement theology (i.e. church replaces Israel). The reason the researcher does not hold to this position is because the church comes through the New Covenant that does not place emphasis upon a person's nationality. Romans 1:16 explained that the gospel is for both the Jew and Gentile.

10. Two references in Matthew that demonstrate that he referred to tax collectors and Gentiles as non-believers are Matthew 5:46-47.

11. Leon Morris, *The Gospel according to Matthew, The Pillar New Testament Commentary* (Grand Rapids, MI; Leicester, England: W.B. Eerdmans; Inter-Varsity Press, 1992), 469.

12. Craig Blomberg, *Matthew, vol. 22, The New American Commentary* (Nashville: Broadman & Holman Publishers, 1992), 279.

13. The explicit truth that the Jerusalem Council confirmed was that the gospel message is for all people. The external nature of man is not a factor on who can have the gospel extended. Both Jews and Greeks are able to receive the gospel. This teaching is confirmed throughout the New Testament: Romans 1:16, Galatians 3:27-28, Ephesians 2:8-9.

14. https://www.barna.com/research/state-church-2016/

15. Graham A. Cole, *He Who Gives Life: The Doctrine of the Holy Spirit, Foundations of Evangelical Theology Series* (Wheaton: Crossway Books, 2007), 224.

16. John Peter Lange et al., *A Commentary on the Holy Scriptures: 1 Corinthians* (Bellingham, WA: Logos Bible Software, 2008), 233.

17. Warren W. Wiersbe, *The Bible Exposition Commentary, vol. 1* (Wheaton, IL: Victor Books, 1996), 605.

18. Michael A.G. Haykin. "'His soul-refreshing presence': The Lord's Supper in Calvinistic Baptist Thought and Experience in the 'Long' Eighteenth Century." In Baptist Sacramentalism. Edited by Anthony R. Cross and Philip E. Thompson. (Carlisle, UK: Paternoster, 2003), 185.

19. J. M. Pendleton, *Baptist Church Manual* (Nashville: Broadman and Holman Publishers, 1966), 89.

20. Ibid., 64.

21. Emphasis added.

22 Dwayne Hastings, "Improper Deacon's Ministry May Stunt Church Growth," accessed March 14 2017, http://www.sbclife.net/Articles/1995/12/sla8.

23. Ibid.

24. Ibid.

25. Ibid.

26. Ibid.

27. This question is taken from Gerald Cowen's book, *Who Rules the Church?*, at which, Cowen seeks to answer the question through examining congregational polity.

28. James Sullivan, Baptist Polity: As I See it (Nashville, TN: Broadman Press, 1983), 51.

29. Ibid.

30. James Leo Garrett, *Systematic Theology: Biblical, Historical, and Evangelical* (North Richland Hills, TX: Bibal Press, 2000), 641. Garrett references the following Baptist authors and their work as using the traditional classifications for church polity: J.M. Pendleton, Church Manual Designed for the Use of Baptist Churches, Hiscox, The New Directory for Baptist Churches, Dargan, Ecclesiology, Dana and Sipes, A Manual of Ecclesiology, and Graces, A Church at Work. Garrett noted that Graves includes another classification in addition to the traditional three by including the "free" polity of the Quakers (641).

31. Ibid.

32. Gerald Cowen, *Who Rules the Church* (Nashville, TN: B&H Publishing Group, 2003), 79. Cowen would later describe the three views under the headings, bishop (episkopoi), elder (presbyters), and congregational (79-85).

33. James Sullivan, *Baptist Polity: As I See It*, 71. The six classifications that Sullivan noted are informal or unstructured, independent and isolationist, hierarchical, delegated, related, and directed and balanced (71-93). Sullivan explained that these are classifications for denominational structures, but he said at times denominational structures are reflected in local churches (71).

34. The two categories that Cowan divides congregationalism into are single-elder congregationalism and plural-elder congregationalism.

35. Millard Erickson, Christian Theology (Grand Rapids, MI:

Baker Academic, 2013), 990.

36. Stephen B. Cowan, *Who Runs the Church? 4 Views on Church Government* (Grand Rapids, MI: Zondervan, 2004), 24. Toon provides his presuppositions in his introductory paragraphs, which indicate that he is writing from an Anglican perspective. Thus, he does not attempt to explain the Roman Catholic understanding of Episcopalianism, though he believes they would fall under the same classification (21).

37. Cowan, *Who Runs the Church?*, 21.

38. Garrett, *Systematic Theology Vol. 1*, 642.

39. Ibid., 642.

40. Ibid., 643. Likewise, Toon would concur with Garrett's assessment of the function of bishops in the Episcopalian tradition. He concludes, as Garrett, that bishops are, "given the care of the whole church, clergy, and laity, as well as the responsibility to teach and defend the faith, supervise worship, administer the sacraments, ordain priests and deacons, and maintain discipline" (35). Such authority was established, according to Toon, during the English Reformation (35).

41. Erickson, *Christian Theology*, 995.

42. R. Laird Harris, "Church, Nature and Government of (Presbyterian View)," in Cohen, Encyclopedia of Christianity, 2:490-92.

43. Erickson explains that, "In the Old Testament the elders were persons who had ruling or governing roles and capacities" (995). Erickson contends that any conversation concerning Presbyterian governance must begin, "with the observation that the Jewish synagogue was ruled by a group of elders, and the Christian, at least initially, functioned within the synagogue" (997).

44. Cowan, Who Runs the Church?, 73. There are some problems with Taylor's presupposition that church polity can be assessed from an Old Testament perspective. The main issue with Taylor's hermeneutic is the establishment of the Christian church did not take form until the New Testament. Thus, to apply Judaism's structure of governance to the church is faulty. Another problem with making a sweeping generalization about church governance is that Judaism's governance is national, meaning that Judaism focuses on the whole

of society, understanding the nation to be a theocracy. Church governance in the New Testament is separate from the societal government. Thus, a New Testament form of church government works within any political governance of a nation.

45. Cowan, *Who Runs the Church?,* 74.

46. Erickson, *Christian Theology*, 996.

47. J. M. Pendleton, *Baptist Church Manual* (Nashville, TN: Broadman Press, 1966), 101. Pendleton's quote comes from his chapter explaining the government of the church. Pendleton presents Presbyterianism as a means of explanation, but he holds to Congregationalism as being the function of government that is explained in the New Testament.

48. Erickson, *Christian Theology*, 996. It is important to note that within Presbyterianism there are great inconsistencies concerning the role of the church member. Erickson points out these inconsistencies through his final paragraph on Presbyterianism. He outlines, what he calls, "critical objections" to Presbyterianism (998). For instance, he cites as one of the objections, the inconsistency of a delegate form of governance for maintaining individual responsibility as a believing church member. He says, "the Presbyterian polity does not give each and every believer an adequate part in church government. While the presbytery and the session are in theory servants and representatives of the individual believers, they may well come to assume a ruling role. Many decisions that could be referred to the church membership as a whole are not. Thus, although intended to represent and carry out the authority of individual believers, the Presbyterian structure of church government has on occasion usurped that authority" (998). Erickson cites Franz Pieper's work, Church Dogmatics, as support for his observations.

49. Because the scope of this paper is to restore congregational polity within Baptist churches, the hermeneutic that will be applied to explaining Congregationalism will be distinctively Baptist.

50. Peter Toon explains the parameters for the Episcopalian form of church government when he says, "Those churches which maintain the historical episcopate claim that their polity is based upon that which developed in the providential guidance of God from the apostolic age through the first few centuries of the Christian church.

For them, this means that it is both wholly in accord with apostolic teaching and take into account the practical results of evangelization, church planting, teaching of the apostles, their fellow workers, and their successors (Who Runs the Church?, 25). As one can see, Episcopalianism utilizes Scripture and Tradition simultaneously to determine proper church governance. Furthermore, Presbyterianism follow the same approach. Taylor describes the hermeneutic employed by Presbyterians for their government when he says, "When we seek to determine what form of church government to adopt, most Christians would turn first to the Bible. But there are other factor to consider as well, such as common sense, culture, Christian wisdom, local circumstances, biblical precedent, and general biblical principles, not just biblical commands and prohibitions (Who Runs the Church?, 74-75). Taylor acquiesces that other factors contribute to polity that are outside of the parameters of Scripture. Reynolds would respond to the hermeneutical approach of Episcopalianism and Presbyterianism by saying, "The Scriptures are a sufficient rule of faith and practice" (Church Polity, 19).

51. Norman, *The Baptist Way*, 85. Emphasis added to demonstrate that the New Testament is the only source for understanding church polity.

52. J. L. Dagg, *Manual of Church Order* (Harrisonburg, VA: Gano Books, 1990), 84.

53. W. T. Connor, *Christian Doctrine* (Nashville, TN: Broadman Press, 1937), 266. Connor explains that the church should function congregationally due to the following two reasons: 1) The New Testament reflects Congregational polity (266), and 2) Christian doctrine necessitates Congregational polity, namely the Lordship of Christ, salvation by grace through faith, and doctrine of the Holy Spirit (267-268).

54. Cowan, *Who Runs the Church?*, 134.

55. Edmund P. Clowney, *The Church* (Downers Grove: InterVarsity, 1995), 202.

56. Jason Duesing, Thomas White, and Malcom Yarnell, III, *Upon This Rock: The Baptist Understanding of the Church* (Nashville, TN: B&H Academic, 2010), 59.

57. Ibid., 117. Garrett utilizes this same definition in his work, Systematic Theology (644).

58. Ibid., 121.

59. Cowen notes that common nomenclature in church-life to-day for the spiritual leader is the term pastor (5). Also, it has been observed, by the writer, that pastor is the common title prescribed in Baptist churches for the spiritual leader. Cowen concedes that the term pastor was most likely not intended to be a title based on his examination of the biblical text; rather the term pastor was used as a description of the function of the spiritual leader in the local church (13).

60. Cowen provides a good argument that demonstrates how shepherd, bishop, and elder are nuances of the same ecclesiastical of-fice. He begins with citing three references (Acts 20, 1 Peter 5, and Titus 1) followed by two logical conclusions. First, he concludes, "pastor, elder, and bishop all refer to the same office. The terms are used interchangeably. Second, "there are two—and only two—per-manent offices in the church: pastor-elder-bishop and deacon. No qualifications are given for any other office" (12-13). Cowen demon-strates that his position stands the test of history by quoting J. B. Lightfoot as saying, "It is a fact now generally recognized by theolo-gians of all shades of opinion, that in the language of the New Tes-tament the same office in the Church is called indifferently 'bishop' (episkopos) and 'elder,' or 'prebyter' (presbuteros)." J.B. Lightfoot, St. Paul's Epistle to the Philippians (London: Macmillan & Co., 1913), 95.

61. William Arndt, Frederick W. Danker, and Walter Bauer, *A Greek-English Lexicon of the New Testament and Other Early Christian Literature* (Chicago: University of Chicago Press, 2000), 230.

62. Pendleton, *The Baptist Church Manual*, 31.

63. The three case studies that will be examined are Acts 6, 13, and 15. There are other passages in the New Testament that are tra-ditionally used to defend Congregationalism. For instance, W. T. Connor cites Matthew 18, Acts 15, and 1 Corinthians 5 (Connor, Christian Doctrine, 266-267). Pendleton cites Matthew 18, Acts 6, Acts 11, Acts 15, 1 Corinthians 5, 2 Corinthians 2, (Pendleton, The Baptist Church Manual, 101-116). Dever, in his chapter in Akin,

Theology for the Church, cites Matthew 18, Acts 6, 1 Corinthians 5, 2 Corinthians 2, Gal 1, and 2 Timothy 4 (Dever, Theology for the Church, 624).

64. John B. Polhill, *Acts, vol. 26, The New American Commentary* (Nashville: Broadman & Holman Publishers, 1992), 178.

65. Norman, *The Baptist Way*, 89.

66. Ibid.

67. Arndt, Danker, and Bauer, *A Greek-English Lexicon*, 129.

68. Doug Redford, *The New Testament Church: Acts-Revelation, vol. 2, Standard Reference Library: New Testament* (Cincinnati, OH: Standard Pub., 2007), 36.

69. Philip A. Bence, *Acts: A Bible Commentary in the Wesleyan Tradition* (Indianapolis, IN: Wesleyan Publishing House, 1998), 78.

70. David G. Peterson, *The Acts of the Apostles, The Pillar New Testament Commentary* (Grand Rapids, MI; Nottingham, England: William B. Eerdmans Publishing Company, 2009), 236.

71. Norman, *The Baptist Way*, 90.

72. John Peter Lange et al., *A Commentary on the Holy Scriptures: Acts* (Bellingham, WA: Logos Bible Software, 2008), 239.

73. Ibid.

74. Much can be said about the doctrinal dispute in Acts 15, but the scope of the paper is to address the way in which the churches handled the dispute not the theological dispute itself.

75. The following argument for congregational polity follows Daniel Akin's argument as presented in R. Stanton Norman's book, The Baptist Way (90-92).

76. Norman, T*he Baptist Way*, 91.

77. Rogers, *Does It Still Matter?*, 192.

Bibliography

Akin, Daniel, *Theology for the Church, Revised Edition*. Nashville, TN: B&H Publishing Group, 2014.

Arndt, William, Frederick W. Danker, and Walter Bauer, *A Greek-English Lexicon of the New Testament and Other Early Christian Literature*. Chicago: University of Chicago Press, 2000.

Barrett, C. K. *The First Epistle to the Corinthians*, Black's New Testament Commentary. London: Continuum, 1968.

Bence, Philip A., *Acts: A Bible Commentary in the Wesleyan Tradition*. Indianapolis, IN: Wesleyan Publishing House, 1998.

Ciampa, Roy E. and Brian S. Rosner, *The First Letter to the Corinthians*, The Pillar New Testament Commentary. Grand Rapids, MI; Cambridge, U.K.: William B. Eerdmans Publishing Company, 2010.

Clowney, Edmund P., *The Church*. Downers Grove: InterVarsity, 1995.

Cole, Graham A. *He Who Gives Life: The Doctrine of the Holy Spirit*. Foundations of Evangelical Theology Series. Wheaton: Crossway Books, 2007.

Connor, W. T., *Christian Doctrine*. Nashville, TN: Broadman Press, 1937.

Crawford, Matthew R. and Thomas R. Schreiner. *The Lord's Supper: Remembering and Proclaiming Christ Until He Comes*, NAC Studies in Bible & Theology. Nashville: B&H Publishing Group, 2010.

Cowan, Stephen B., *Who Runs the Church? 4 Views on Church Government*. Grand Rapids, MI: Zondervan, 2004.

Cowen, Gerald., *Who Rules the Church*. Nashville, TN: B&H Publishing Group, 2003.

Dagg, J. L., *Manual of Church Order*. Harrisonburg, VA: Gano Books, 1990.

Dagg, J. L. *Manual of Theology: A Treatise on Church Order*. Harrisonburg: Gano Books, 1990.

Duesing, Jason, Thomas White, and Malcom Yarnell, III, *Upon The Rock: The Baptist Understanding of the Church*. Nashville, TN: B&H Academic, 2010.

Ellingworth, Paul, Howard Hatton, and Paul Ellingworth, *A Handbook on Paul's First Letter to the Corinthians*, UBS Handbook Series. New York: United Bible Societies, 1995.

Erickson, Millard, *Christian Theology*. Grand Rapids, MI: Baker Academic, 2013.

Garrett, James Leo, *Systematic Theology: Biblical, Historical, and Evangelical*. North Richland Hills, TX: Bibal Press, 2000.

Harris, R. Laird, "Church, Nature and Government of (Presbyterian View)," in Cohen, *Encyclopedia of Christianity*, 2:490-92.

Hastings, Dwayne, "Improper Deacon's Ministry May Stunt Church Growth," accessed March 14 2017. http://www.sbclife.net/Articles/1995/12/sla8.

Haykin. Michael A. G. "'His soul-refreshing presence': The Lord's Supper in Calvinistic Baptist Thought and Experience in the 'Long' Eighteenth Century." In *Baptist Sacramentalism*. Edited by Anthony R. Cross and Philip E. Thompson. Carlisle, UK: Paternoster, 2003.

Johnson, Alan F. *1 Corinthians*, vol. 7, The IVP New Testament Commentary Series. Downers Grove, IL: InterVarsity Press, 2004.

Lange, John Peter et al., *A Commentary on the Holy Scriptures: Acts*. Bellingham, WA: Logos Bible Software, 2008.

Lange, Peter et al., *A Commentary on the Holy Scriptures: 1 Corinthians*. Bellingham, WA: Logos Bible Software, 2008.

Lenski, R. C. H. *The Interpretation of St. Paul's First and Second Epistle to the Corinthians*. Minneapolis, MN: Augsburg Publishing House, 1963.

Lightfoot, J.B., *St. Paul's Epistle to the Philippians*. London: Macmillan & Co., 1913.

Pendleton, J. M. *Baptist Church Manual*. Nashville: Broadman and Holman Publishers, 1966.

Peterson, David G., *The Acts of the Apostles*, The Pillar New Testament Commentary. Grand Rapids, MI; Nottingham, England: William B. Eerdmans Publishing Company, 2009.

Piper, Franz, *Church Dogmatics*. Concordia Publishing House, 2003.

Polhill, John B., *Acts*, vol. 26, The New American Commentary. Nashville: Broadman & Holman Publishers, 1992.

Redford, Doug, *The New Testament Church: Acts-Revelation*, vol. 2, Standard Reference Library: New Testament. Cincinnati, OH: Standard Pub., 2007.

Sullivan, James, *Baptist Polity: As I See it*. Nashville, TN: Broadman Press, 1983.

Spence-Jones, H. D. M. ed., *1 Corinthians*, The Pulpit Commentary. London; New York: Funk & Wagnalls Company, 1909.

Thiselton, Anthony C. *The First Epistle to the Corinthians: A Commentary on the Greek Text*, New International Greek Testament Commentary. Grand Rapids, MI: W.B. Eerdmans, 2000.

Utley, Robert James. *Paul's Letters to a Troubled Church: I and II Corinthians*, vol. Volume 6, Study Guide Commentary Series. Marshall, TX: Bible Lessons International, 2002.

Wiersbe, Warren W. *The Bible Exposition Commentary*, vol. 1. Wheaton, IL: Victor Books, 1996.

About the Author

Timothy Pigg serves as the lead pastor of Fellowship Church, with campuses in Immokalee and Ave Maria in southwest Florida. His work and ministry has allowed him to serve in many local church contexts over the last 14 years. This has birthed in Timothy a love for the local church, ecclesiology, and text-driven preaching and practice.

A native of Jacksonville, Florida, Timothy had the incredible privilege of growing up under the expositional preaching of Dr. Jerry Vines and attending the yearly Jacksonville Pastor's Conference. Timothy moved to Texas and studied under Dr. Paige Patterson at Southwestern Baptist Theological Seminary in Fort Worth for seven years, earning a Bachelor's of Arts in Humanities (2013), a Master of Divinity (2015), and a Doctorate in Ministry (2020). While at Southwestern, Timothy served as an assistant under Dr. Waylan Owens in the School of Education. Timothy also served on staff in several local churches in North Texas.

In 2020, Timothy joined together with several pastors and laymen throughout the Southern Baptist Convention to launch the Conservative Baptist Network — a group focused on maintaining a longstanding, convention-wide commitment to the inerrancy and sufficiency of Scripture. He serves on the Conservative Baptist Network Steering Council, coordinates State Chapters, and is editor of the *Conservative Baptist Bulletin.*

In 2021, Timothy launched the Text-Driven Podcast, dedicated to equipping believers to know God and make Him known through text-driven preaching and practice.

Timothy is married to Jessica, a writer for the Florida Baptist Convention, Conservative Baptist Network Press, and contributor to *The Devotional for Women*, *The Devotional for Women: Psalms & Proverbs*, and the *Daily Devotional Bible for Women.* The two have called sunny, southwest Florida home since May 2015.

CPSIA information can be obtained
at www.ICGtesting.com
Printed in the USA
JSHW040305271222
35263JS00004B/164